i told me so

i told

me so

Self-Deception and
the Christian Life

Gregg A. Ten Elshof

WILLIAM B. EERDMANS PUBLISHING COMPANY
GRAND RAPIDS, MICHIGAN / CAMBRIDGE, U.K.

Published 2009 by
WM. B. EERDMANS PUBLISHING CO.
2140 Oak Industrial Drive N.E., Grand Rapids, Michigan 49505 /
P.O. Box 163, Cambridge CB3 9PU U.K.
www.eerdmans.com

Printed in the United States of America

14 13 12 11 10   7 6 5 4 3 2

Library of Congress Cataloging-in-Publication Data

Ten Elshof, Gregg, b. 1970 –
I told me so : self-deception and the Christian life / Gregg A. Ten Elshof.
        p.   cm.
    ISBN 978-0-8028-6411-6 (pbk. : alk. paper)
    1. Self-deception — Religious aspects — Christianity.
    2. Christian life. I. Title

BV4267.F3T46   2009
241'.673 — dc22

                                      2009012686

Scripture quotations are from the New Revised Standard Version Bible, copyright
1989, Division of Christian Education of the National Council of the Churches of
Christ in the United States of America. Used by permission. All rights reserved.

To Thursday

(even when it falls on a Wednesday)

Contents

Foreword

I N HIS TEACHINGS JESUS Christ picked up on a note struck by the prophet Isaiah: "This people honors me with their lips, but their heart is far away from me" (Mark 7:6, Isaiah 29:13). The apostle Paul famously remarked upon the incongruity between what he wanted to do and what he actually did (Romans 7:15). Jeremiah stood in amazement before the deceitfulness of the human heart. He judged it to be "desperately sick" and inscrutable to the human mind. He as well as the Psalmist could only look to God to penetrate its murky depths (Jeremiah 17:9-10, Psalm 139:23-24). Current events easily suggest that not that much has changed since ancient days, and the tenor of the usual Christian landscape seems to match up pretty well with what Jesus and the prophets saw.

There is not much use in getting indignant about this. It is really too important to spend much time attacking it, for attacks do little to help or change the situation. Transformation of believers into disciples clothed with inner and outer Christlikeness has increasingly become a matter of concern for Christians and Christian leaders in recent years, and the dynamics of personal inconsistency, individually and in groups, must be understood and practically mastered if anything like the clear patterns of Christlike living, familiar from the New Testament, are to be realized.

Self-deception is a major part of what defeats spiritual formation in Christ. In self-deception the individual or group refuses to acknowledge factors in their life of which they are dimly conscious, or even know to be the case, but are unprepared to deal with: to openly admit and take steps to change. As a result, those factors continue to govern their actions and shape their thoughts and emotions. The further result is that what they *say* they believe, intend, and want is not borne out in life. The vehement affirmations of Peter and the other disciples that they would not desert Christ are peculiarly vivid illustrations of how self-deception works, but the dreary details of daily life constantly confirm that this type of failure is not just for "religious" affairs. It pervades every area of human existence.

One of the worst mistakes we can make in coming to grips with these well-known human failures is to think of them solely in terms of will and "will power." Of course the will is involved, but the will is not what immediately governs the "normal" life. Such a life is controlled by inertia, habit, bent of character — stuff we really don't pay much attention to, if any at all, and in some cases "stuff" we don't even recognize or admit is a part of "us." The self that does the deceiving in self-deception is this inertial bulk of habit and bent of character, embedded in our body and its social relations, ready to go without thinking or choice. That was what Jesus knew to be the case with Peter and his associates, and it will be the same with us unless we have truly stepped into the light. The will — the ability to initiate change — is of course central to change, and *it* must change. But it can do that only if it comes to grips with the realities of all else that is in us and finds means and grace to change how *we really do* think and feel, how we live our social relationships, and what our body is poised to do before we start thinking about it.

Paul the apostle challenges us to "walk as children of light; for the fruit of the light consists in all goodness and righteousness and truth" (Ephesians 5:8-9). And we can do that. It is something for us to do. It will not be done *for* us or *to* us — though help will come. We have to understand what self-deception is, how it works its subtle control, and steps that can be taken to defeat it.

Here is where this book comes in. Gregg Ten Elshof has done a masterful job of showing how people manage to do the strange and sometimes dreadful things they do — often directly contrary to their self-professed thoughts, feelings, and intentions. He makes clear how the realities of mind, body, and soul work against conscious and sincere declarations, and how individuals fail themselves by failing to deal honestly with what is in them. That is the nature and the effect of self-deception. And then he guides us into what we can do to defeat self-deception.

Ten Elshof's discussions are erudite, biblical, searching, and laced with soul-restoring wisdom. All of this together means that this book is solidly pastoral. What it brings to us is appropriate to individuals, but it especially belongs in the context of small groups and local congregations that are earnestly set upon growing together in Christ. It is written with a clarity and style that makes its deepest teachings accessible to everyone. The aspirations of lovers of Christ to live in the light with him, to be children of light indeed, will find effectual guidance on the pages of this book.

Dallas Willard
University of Southern California

Preface

A MOTHER SOMEHOW MANAGES not to notice the obvious signs that her son is on drugs. A wife does the same with respect to her husband's affair. All of the evidence is easily available. Yet it goes unseen. The young man puts out of mind the horrors of the sex-slave industry driving the pornography business and convinces himself that these women actually enjoy their work. The politician convinces himself that his lofty ends justify morally ambiguous means (or worse). The director of a Christian non-profit organization manages to find sincerely compelling a perspective from which money donated to the ministry can legitimately be used to pay for an extravagant personal vacation or, perhaps, a private jet.

This book is about self-deception. It's about the amazing human capacity to break free from the constraints of rationality when truth ceases to be the primary goal of inquiry. Beginning with the Scriptures themselves, self-deception looms large in the historical attempt to explain and describe Christian experience. But there is precious little in contemporary Christian writing by way of sustained focus on the role of self-deception in the Christian life. This book intends to fill that void.

More accurately, this book intends to put something in the void. To fill the void is too ambitious a task. I don't say anything close to everything that can and should be said about self-deception. But I hope I say enough to enable you to entertain seriously the possibility that, for better or worse, self-deception is a part of your life. You can either pretend it's not there — which is to add yet another layer of it — or you can turn and consider it explicitly. The aim of this book is to help you begin to do the latter.

Chapter one introduces self-deception and explains why otherwise sane, rational, and good people engage in self-deception. The chapter also explains the disappearance of self-deception from the contemporary discussion of Christian living in terms of the recent emphasis on the virtue of authenticity. Chapter two explains in more detail what self-deception is. It explores the relationship between interpersonal deception and self-deception and suggests that we are self-deceived whenever we manage our own beliefs for the sake of some goal other than the truth. Chapters three and four introduce five of the main strategies for successfully deceiving yourself. For each strategy, there is a general description and explanation followed by an exploration of what I hope are recognizable manifestations of the strategy in the Christian life in particular.

Chapter five explores the social aspect of self-deception. Often we work as a team to keep each other in the dark. Once again, a general description of the phenomenon of "groupthink" is followed by an exploration of how it shows up in Christian culture. Chapters six and seven explain how to move progressively away from vicious self-deception. Surprisingly, an important step in moving away from vicious self-deception is the realization that self-deception is not always such a bad idea — that it can serve legitimate purposes. After explaining the positive contribution of self-deception and the mechanisms that give rise to it, three pieces of advice are offered for moving progressively away from the kinds of self-deception that do us harm. Finally, chapter eight warns against postures that can be the result of having thought about self-deception. This topic, like many others, is a dangerous one. An exploration of self-deception can too easily result in cynicism, self-doubt, or a vicious sort of hyper-authenticity. Chapter eight is intended to forestall these errors.

To whom can you safely dedicate a book on self-deception? I suppose the last thing anybody wants is to be mentioned in a book of this sort — much less to be the object of its dedication. I've had great fun in recent months telling friends and family that I'm writing a book on self-deception and that they're in it. "In fact," I'll sometimes add, "I've considered dedicating the book to you and using your name as the subtitle." Nobody seems particularly flattered, honored, or excited about that possibility. For a time, I thought of dedicating the book to myself. I'm most familiar with my own self-deceptive strategies, after all, and this would spare everyone else the embarrassment. But then who am *I* to say that I'm most familiar with my own self-deceptive strategies. Maybe I'm not. Maybe I'm self-deceived in the belief that I am. I can't confidently dedicate the book even to me. So I've decided to dedicate the book to a day of the week. More on that shortly.

First, though, heartfelt thanks are in order. Thanks to those who've read early drafts of the book in whole or part and have been willing to spend their time in conversation with me about it: Paul Buchanan, Don Carr, David Ciocchi, Tom Crisp, Roger Freet, Andy McGuire, Brad Monsma, Steve Porter, Dave Rhode, Paul Spears, Gene and Judy Ten Elshof, Laurel Ten Elshof, and Dallas Willard.

Special thanks to David Bratt for the patience it takes, no doubt, to edit the work of a philosopher, and for rescuing the book from itself. Thanks to Todd Picket and Jack Schwarz for working hard to find release time for me to make this project possible. Thanks to Roger Freet for guiding me patiently through unfamiliar waters. Thanks to my neighborhood community for embodying several of the ideals that find expression in this book. And thanks most of all to Laurel, Silas, Larkin, and Gideon for the life we share together. The energy to write and think feels like overflow from the life of joy and peace I have with you.

Finally, though, the book is dedicated to a day of the week: Thursday. For over fifteen years, God has used Thursday more than any other day to teach me about self-deception and to help me come to grips with my own self-deceptive strategies. On Thursdays, I've learned by experience about diverse and safe community and I've had the opportunity to practice Christ-likeness with others. On Thursdays, I've learned that I am loveable even when I'm known nearly all the way through. For better or worse, I would not be who I am today were it not for that day of the week. So, by extension, were it not for that day of the week, this book would never have been written.

CHAPTER 1

Let's Make a Deal

The Offer

I'M A COLLEGE PROFESSOR — I have been for almost a decade. I work reasonably hard at my job, and I think I do it fairly well. In fact, in my honest and solitary moments, when there's no occasion for false humility, I'd say I'm a better-than-average teacher.

I'm in good company. A recent study revealed that 94 percent of the people who do what I do think they're doing a better-than-average job. And it's not just college professors. "A survey of one million high-school seniors found that 70 percent thought they were above average in leadership ability, and only 2 percent thought they were below average. In terms of ability to get along with others, *all* students thought they were above average, 60 percent thought they were in the top 10 percent, and 25 percent thought they were in the top 1 percent!"[1] Clearly, a lot of people are wrong about how they stack up in comparison with their peers.

Fortunately, I'm not one of them. Am I?

---

1. See Thomas Gilovich, *How We Know What Isn't So* (New York: Free Press, 1991), p. 77.

What's going on? These are intelligent and often self-reflective people. Many of them are aware of statistics like the ones I've just cited. For some of them, the evidence against the suggestion that they're doing a better-than-average job is fairly straightforward. Still they persist in their belief. They discount or ignore the evidence suggesting less-than-stellar job performance (negative course evaluations, people falling asleep in class, low course enrollments, bad test results) and find unusual standards against which to judge their work. But they seem utterly oblivious to the fact that they're doing this. They are the victims of a completely successful sham and deserve our pity. Except for the fact that there's nobody to blame for the lie but *them*. If they're to blame, should we still pity them?

But who *can* blame them, really? They've got an amazingly good thing going when you stop to think about it. It's hard work being a *genuinely* better-than-average college professor. It's hard to engage thoughtfully with the forty-third paper in the stack on Plato's *Republic* — most of them written in the wee hours of the morning they were due. It's hard work getting to know the quiet student — the one who sits in the middle of the far left side of the classroom — to get to know her well enough to really help her along with her thinking. Connecting with students often means time with them beyond what we do together in the classroom — a movie night to discuss *The Matrix* at your house on a Wednesday night, say, or attending the Collegiate Cheese Club society meeting that *begins* after you're usually in bed.

And what do you get in return for your effort? There isn't much money in it. And if your field is relatively obscure (mine's philosophy), you can forget about fame. At best, you get to go through life with a certain *satisfaction* in the realization that your job is important and you're doing it well. But suppose you could have that same experience of satisfaction without all the hard work of becoming (and continuing to be) a *genuinely* better-than-average college professor? If you could convince yourself that you were better than average, you could enjoy all the benefits of theft over honest toil. The one catch is that you'd have to do all of this convincing without catching yourself in the act. If you caught yourself in the lie, you'd miss out on the satisfaction that comes from believing, really believing, that you're doing a better-than-average job.

So lots of college professors have taken the deal. And it's not terribly shocking that they have. It is, after all, a pretty good deal. What *is* surprising is that they are able to pull it off — that they are able to tell themselves the lie without catching themselves in the act. And what's alarming is that if I had taken the deal, it would seem to me (as it *does in fact* seem to me) that I had not.

As it turns out, a fair bit of our felt well-being is dependent on our beliefs. In this case, what I believe about my job performance has a direct bearing on my sense of well-being. I feel better when I believe that I'm doing my job well. But other beliefs affect my well-being too. I believe that I'm in a vibrant, growing marriage with a beautiful woman who has been (and continues to be) faithful to me, that I have friendships that are — some of them, anyway — deeper and richer than your average friendship, and that my friends and my wife love me with something that approximates unconditional love. I believe that I'm relatively free of egregious racial bias — the kind that leads people to think reprehensible thoughts about and do reprehensible things to each other. I believe that I've successfully come over from being a "non-Christian" to being a "Christian" and that I'm making some progress toward maturity in Christ. I believe that God's not presently calling me to missionary work in Africa and that if he did call me to missionary work in Africa — if it was a very, *very* clear call — I'd go (or at least I'd seriously consider it). I believe that I can honestly sign the doctrinal statement that you have to sign in order to work at the Christian institution where I teach — that I really do believe everything it says I believe. These are just a few of the beliefs that contribute noticeably to my sense of well-being. There are many more.

Each of these beliefs offers me a certain kind of satisfaction. A discovery to the effect that I was in error about any of them would be pretty upsetting. If I discovered that the seeming depth of my friendships was a sham, I would be significantly disappointed. If it dawned on me that my marriage had been stagnant (or worse) for the last decade, I would be crushed and disillusioned. A discovery to the effect that I could not honestly sign that doctrinal statement would be a source of deep anxiety and fear about my future job prospects. To discover that I'd not been making any progress in the last ten years toward maturity in Christ would depress me to no end. And what would it say about me if I were *not* ready to go to Africa if God really did call me there?

Here again, life offers me a deal. The beliefs I have about myself and others do not need to be *true* to bring me satisfaction. I only need to *believe* them. Sustaining depth of friendship is hard work — as is growing in Christ. Our best counselors tell us that unguarded marriages trend toward stagnation or worse, and I suppose one doesn't become the kind of person that can drop everything and follow God's call to Africa overnight. If I could somehow convince myself that I were succeeding on each of these fronts, I could enjoy all of the benefits of theft over honest toil. Again, the one catch is that I'd have to convince myself that these successes are truly successes without catching myself in the act. If I caught myself ignoring or mishandling evidence toward this end, the game would be up and I'd miss out on the opportunity to believe, really believe, all of these things it gives me such deep satisfaction to believe.

So it shouldn't be a shock to discover that many have taken the deal with respect to beliefs like these. In fact, most of us could identify people (*other* people, of course) who've done just exactly that. We call them "self-deceived," and we feel a mixture of pity and reproach for them. Again, it's not so surprising that there are folks who take the deal. What's surprising is that they're able to pull it off — that they can manage to *actually* believe these things in the face of evidence (obvious to everyone but them) to the contrary. And what's alarming is that, had I taken the deal, it would seem to me (as it *does in fact* seem to me) that I had not.

Self-Deception in the Christian Tradition

Philosophers, social scientists, and psychologists have long been aware of the pervasive reality of self-deception. For centuries, it has been called upon to explain various forms of irrationality and dysfunction. Interestingly, it has also been called upon to explain survival and success in a variety of contexts. Historically, few masters of Christian spirituality have failed to notice the significance of self-deception. Christian thinkers through the ages have had a special interest in the bearing of self-deception on the Christian life and the pursuit of — or flight from — God, and it has long served as a key element in the explanation of sin, moral failure, and the avoidance of God.

The prophet Jeremiah reminds us that the heart is deceitful

above all things and asks, rhetorically, "who can understand it?" (Jeremiah 17:9). The prophet Obadiah identifies a primary motive for self-deception: "Your proud heart has deceived you . . ." (Obadiah 3). The apostle Paul explains in his letter to the Galatians how self-deception enables those who are nothing to think that they are something (Galatians 6:3), and in his rather depressing description of the flight from God in the first chapter of his letter to the Romans, he gives us the following:

> For the wrath of God is revealed from heaven against all ungodliness and wickedness of those who by their wickedness *suppress the truth*. For what can be known about God *is plain to them*, because God has shown it to them. Ever since the creation of the world his eternal power and divine nature, invisible though they are, have been understood and seen through the things he has made. So *they are without excuse;* for though they knew God they did not honor him as God or give thanks to him, but they became futile in their thinking, and *their senseless minds were darkened.* (Romans 1:18-21, emphasis added)

In his first pastoral letter, John calls on the language of self-deception in an attempt to explain our flight from repentance: "If we say that we have no sin, we deceive ourselves, and the truth is not in us" (1 John 1:8). Thomas Aquinas picks up the theme and suggests that "ignorance is sometimes directly and intrinsically voluntary, as when one freely chooses to be ignorant so that he may sin more freely."[2] For Bishop Joseph Butler, an eighteenth-century

2. Thomas Aquinas, *Summa Theologiae* (New York: McGraw-Hill, 1964), vol. 25, 155.

philosopher and theologian, the "self-flattering forms of self-deception" explain a great deal of the wickedness that we encounter in the world. So significant is the danger of self-deception for Butler that he devotes three of his major sermons to the topic.[3]

Strangely, though, sustained discussion of the human propensity towards self-deception has all but disappeared from twentieth-century analyses of the spiritual life. There are, of course, still specialists in philosophy and psychology working out the details. But, for most of us, self-deception simply doesn't jump immediately to mind as a significant element in the explanation of our experience. We rarely think of it. Lots of people I talk to have never so much as considered the possibility that they've fallen prey to it in any significant way. One is reminded here of the haunting suggestion in Bishop Butler's tenth sermon that "those who have never had any suspicion of, who have never made allowances for this weakness in themselves, who have never (if I may be allowed such a manner of speaking) caught themselves in it, may almost take it for granted that they have been very much misled by it."

Deceiving Ourselves About Self-Deception

What happened? How did we lose sight of this phenomenon that plays such a significant role in the historical understanding of Christian experience? For reasons that will become clearer as we move forward, understanding how we lost sight of self-deception

3. For a less brief survey of these thinkers, see Mike Martin's excellent book *Self-Deception and Morality* (Lawrence: University Press of Kansas, 1986), esp. chapter 3.

will position us nicely to reconsider it. Paradoxically, it was a historical *overe*mphasis on self-deception as a moral vice that led to its disappearance from the horizon of our conscious self-awareness. Put differently, it's because we made too big a deal of it that we stopped thinking of it altogether.

Until recently, Christian thinkers have warned against self-deception primarily because of its ability to facilitate more serious sin. There is a kind of wrongdoing which is possible only *after* you've convinced yourself to believe certain things — that a greater good is served, that the people you're mistreating somehow deserve it (or aren't *really* persons at all), that the pain you're causing is less severe than it is, that you have no viable alternatives, and the list goes on. As Mike Martin explains,

> Evading self-acknowledgment of our faults enables us to avoid painful moral emotions: guilt and remorse for harming others; shame for betraying our own ideals; self-contempt for not meeting even our minimal commitments. We also bypass the sometimes onerous task of abiding by our values and manage to sin freely and pleasurably. We avoid the need to make amends and restitution for the harm we do. And, above all, we maintain a flattering self-image while pursuing immoral ends, often in the name of virtue.[4]

Martin goes on to illustrate the point with reference to the memoirs of Albert Speer, Hitler's powerful minister of armaments and war production. Speer was a "talented architect and bureaucrat, a loving family man, and considerate to his circle of

4. Martin, *Self-Deception and Morality*, pp. 37, 38.

peers."[5] How, then, could he possibly bring himself to the assigning of prisoners to the torture of Auschwitz? In his own telling of it, Speer refused to investigate the happenings at Auschwitz and elsewhere. He diverted his attention so thoroughly and systematically as to render psychologically manageable what would have been morally unthinkable if confronted squarely. Life cut him a deal: refuse to be convinced that the goings-on at Auschwitz are monstrous — believe instead that they're not so bad as all that — and you can experience the satisfaction that comes from believing that *you're* not a moral monster. He took the deal.

Closer to where we live, consider John, a nineteen-year-old Christian college student who spends considerable energy organizing his day with an eye toward getting time alone with his computer in his dorm room. If he's at all globally aware, he has good reason to think there may be some connection between the pornography he's consuming and the global sex-slave crisis that feeds the industry. But he's a morally decent person with basically normal moral sensitivities. If he fully acknowledged the horrific realities of the slave trade responsible for the production of images like the ones he's consuming, he couldn't live with himself — or the images would no longer serve their intended purpose. There are those, of course, who've tragically lost even this basic level of moral sensitivity. For them, no self-deception is needed; they can live with themselves in full conscious recognition of their contribution to the industry of sexual slavery. Ironically, though, it is precisely the *genuine* moral sensitivity of the average consumer that creates the need for self-deceiving ignorance of the causal history of the pornography he consumes. So life cuts him a deal: refuse to

5. Martin, *Self-Deception and Morality*, p. 38.

be convinced that there is a tight connection between *these* images and the horrors of the sex-slave industry — believe instead that *these* images were created in morally neutral circumstances — and you can experience the satisfaction that comes from believing that you've not been complicit in those horrors.

So, to be sure, self-deception often facilitates significant wrongdoing.

An interesting thing happened, though, with the rise in prominence of the philosophical movement called *existentialism*. Existentialism is notoriously difficult to define to everyone's satisfaction — and, fortunately, it needn't be defined precisely for the purposes of this discussion. Only this much of it needs to be understood: beginning with Kierkegaard, the existentialists (including Sartre, Schopenhauer, Nietzsche, and others) elevated *authenticity* to a place of primary importance in their understanding of the virtues. Due to the writings of the existentialists and other cultural trends, the "Good Person" was increasingly understood to be the "Authentic Person." Being true to oneself became a — or, in some cases, *the* — chief good. Self-deception, then, was given a promotion in the ranking of vices. What was once a derivative vice — one whose primary importance was found in its ability to facilitate other, more serious, vices — became itself the most egregious of all sins.

Now a remarkable thing happens when a vice gets a promotion, when it is perceived as having greater negative moral weight than it once had. Consider racism. Many of us, myself included, have a hard time these days admitting that we correlate the significance of a person's existence with the color of his or her skin. It hasn't always been so. There have been times and places — in fact, there are places now — where people would have no trouble at all recognizing that they correlate the significance of a person's existence with the color of his or her skin. They may or may not use the word, but they have no trouble with the idea that they are, themselves, racists.

In the recent history of developed western society, though, racism earned a well-deserved promotion in the ordering of vices. This is all to the good. But with that promotion came an increased emotional cost in the recognition, "I am a racist." If racism is worse than we thought, then it's harder than it used to be to admit to yourself that you're a racist. And it is at this point that life offers us the self-deception deal. You can experience the satisfaction that rightly belongs to the person who steers clear of the vice of racism if you can but convince yourself that you're not a racist. Unsurprisingly, a great many people take the deal. What's surprising is that they're able to pull it off. And what's alarming is that if I've taken the deal, it will seem to me (as it *does in fact* seem to me) that I have not.

So, whenever a particular vice gets a promotion in the ordering of vices, the temptation to be self-deceived about the fact that one exhibits that vice increases. And, with the rise of existentialism and the supreme value of *authenticity*, self-deception got a promotion in the ordering of vices. And so, paradoxically, the vice of self-deception has been increasingly veiled from view by its own machinations.

For better or worse, authenticity continues to be a supreme value in contemporary western Christian culture. In fact, it seems still to be on the rise. Last year, when I served on a committee to review candidates for my college's presidency, one of the most interesting things I learned was that there is a significant generation gap when it comes to the ranking of qualities that make for good leaders. Recent studies indicate that when asked for the top five qualities needed to be a good leader, those older than fifty place competency at the top of the list, but for college-aged adults, authenticity is chief among the qualifications. This is a remarkable shift.

I'm aware of it in my classroom. Students don't want simply to be handed the information requisite for competence in their field. They want to know *me* — the "real" me. In church, folks want to hear from a pastor who is "real." They bristle against preaching that feels "canned" or that comes off like a performance. Preachers who work hard to craft language that does justice to their sermon topic put themselves at risk of disapproval along these lines. Pastors who are comfortable making mistakes and presenting their audience with an "unpolished" talk score points on the authenticity scale and are — all other things being equal — approved on that basis.

Now I don't mean to say that authenticity is a bad thing, or that we should embrace hypocrisy and phony leadership. The present emphasis on authenticity is at least in part a legitimate reaction to an overabundance of phony leadership in recent decades. A colleague of mine once described today's young-ish church population as having "hyper-sensitive B.S. detectors." And there's nothing wrong with the ability to detect and root out B.S. The world could get by with considerably less of it, to be sure.

But my point is that the elevation of "authenticity" as a virtue carries with it a promotion for self-deception among the vices. So, to the degree that we value authenticity, we will be averse to the suggestion that we are self-deceived. Believing myself to be authentic — to be true to myself and to others — will be a source of significant satisfaction and felt well-being for me. But, as it turns out, being *genuinely* honest with oneself is often hard work. And it is at this point that life cuts us a deal. If we can convince ourselves that we're authentic people — that we're not self-deceived — we can have all the benefit of theft over honest toil. We can experience the satisfaction associated with saying, "Whatever else is true of me, I'm honest with myself and with others. I know myself. I'm real."

As we'll see in later chapters, a major strategy for the self-deceiver is simple subject avoidance. We simply resist attentive focus on the painful topic and are thereby enabled to persist in our belief. So we resist the topic of self-deception.

Earlier I quoted scholars from centuries ago on this topic, but we find precious little sustained focus in recent Christian literature on the phenomenon of self-deception. My hope in this book is to bring self-deception squarely into view as an object of attention. What is this phenomenon, exactly? Can we be any more precise than we've been already about the conditions under which it regularly occurs? To what extent are these conditions realized in contemporary western Christian subcultures? Is it always a vice, or does it sometimes serve legitimate ends? To the extent that it is a vice, how bad is it, and why is it bad? How can we identify it in our own case? What are the typical forms that it takes? In particular, how does it manifest itself in Christian subcultures? And what can we do about it?

Ironically, if we hope to bring self-deception back into focus as an important element in the explanation of our lived Christian experience, we may need to give it a demotion in the order of vices. The ability to take oneself into deception is, after all, an amazing (and presumably God-given) ability. Is it conceivable that there are legitimate ends for this remarkable ability? Might it have a legitimate purpose?

CHAPTER 2

What? Why? Where?

The Complexity of Belief

M OST PEOPLE THINK FAR too simplistically about their beliefs. We think we either have them or we don't. We speak of
beliefs as though one can, for the most part, simply decide to have
them or not. And we assume that each person is the unquestion-
able authority on the question of which beliefs he or she has.

When I teach on the topic of belief, I always begin by having
my students consider the following three sentences, taking note of
which ones come out true for them if stated in the first person.

1.   I have lots and lots and LOTS of beliefs.
2.   I believe that some of my beliefs are false.
3.   It's fairly likely that I don't believe all of the things I think I
     believe.

The first one usually comes easily. Most students are immediately
ready to acknowledge the fact that they have lots of beliefs. When I
ask them for examples, most of them cite first the beliefs that seem
important to them — that God exists, that murder is immoral, that

the war in Iraq is justified or unjustified, and so on. But these beliefs about "important" topics are just the tip of the iceberg.

Sometimes I ask students to give an estimate as to the percentage of their own beliefs they've consciously considered in the past week. Initial estimates are almost always radically high (3 percent? 1 percent?). Then I ask them to consider just their beliefs about numbers. How many believe that 7×7=49 or that 6−4=2? Or about presidents: How many believe that George Washington was the first president of the United States, or that Abraham Lincoln was assassinated?

We have a huge stock of beliefs, and most of them lie dormant in memory. We've not considered them for ages, but they're there, just beyond consciousness, ready to be called up in an instant. If you're the type who can stare up at the stars and get lost in wonder at the sheer number of them, try also considering the sheer number of your own beliefs. It's an unfathomably large collection.

We share many of these beliefs in common, and one of the most important and interesting things about you is which of them you bring to conscious attention on a regular basis. Which do you spend time with? Which do you allow to go unconsidered for large stretches of time?

Consider now the second sentence: Some of my beliefs are false. Students tend to be slightly slower in acknowledging the truth of this sentence. If they don't stop to reflect, they're likely to be of the opinion that all of their beliefs are true. But usually they can be brought around to the recognition that there are false beliefs sneaking around somewhere in their psyche. After all, they've been wrong about things before. Just yesterday, I had a false belief about where my car was parked in the parking lot. Of course, I don't have *that* belief anymore. But isn't it a little presumptuous to think that yesterday was the last time I'll ever discover that I've believed something false? We bump into false belief all the time, and there's no good reason to think it's now happened for the very last time.

Another reason to think that some of my beliefs might be false is that I haven't even so much as considered most of them for ages. I've got beliefs that I formed when I was a grade-schooler and haven't really considered since. A little while ago, my son Silas was stung by a bee. He asked me what would happen to the bee now that the stinger had been lodged in his finger. I immediately and confidently responded that the bee would die (hoping privately that the death would be slow and excruciating). But I hadn't considered that question since I was a small child. I can't even remember where I learned it. From a book? A teacher? A neighborhood friend? How trustworthy was the source? Is it true of all bees (including the one that just stung Silas?) or just a specific kind located where I grew up? Reflecting on the conditions under which I likely formed this belief, I found myself slowly becoming less confident in its truth. Many of my beliefs have been formed under less than ideal circumstances and haven't been considered since. How confident should I be that they're true? Almost certainly, some of them are false.

So, sentence (2) seems true. I've got false beliefs swimming around in my consciousness somewhere or other. But which ones? Interestingly, reflective people will exhibit confidence that they've got false beliefs, but they'll be unable to give you a single concrete example. It's one thing to say you've got false beliefs; it's quite another to cite a particular false belief as one that you nevertheless have. It's easy to cite examples of false belief that I *used to* have. I used to believe that my car was parked over *there* but now I see that it's not. So I don't believe that anymore. But it's quite another thing to cite an example of a false belief you've still got. And if you tried, we might worry. Why, after all, would you not have abandoned the belief upon seeing that it's false?

So there is this trouble with belief: I'm convinced that I've got false beliefs, but each of my beliefs, when I consider it, seems true to me. How, one might wonder, am I ever supposed to locate my false beliefs when each of them looks true to me?

But that's not the end of trouble. Consider sentence (3): "It's fairly likely that I don't believe all of the things I think I believe." It's not just that I'm sometimes wrong about whether my belief is true; I'm sometimes wrong about whether or not I even have the belief in question! Students are generally most reluctant about this one. How could I possibly be wrong about this? If I think I believe that George Washington was the first president, it seems as sure as anything that I *do* believe that George Washington was the first president (even if, as things turn out, he wasn't). How could I come to think that I believe something that I don't believe?

This is the question that gives rise to the problem of self-deception. Consider again the person with racist beliefs. Lucille is a dear Christian woman in her eighties. Suppose Lucille is answering a series of True/False questions and comes upon the following:

True or false: People of all ethnicities are equally valuable, equally loved by God, and equally to be respected.

Lucille would circle "true" without hesitation. It would strike her as a truism — something you'd have to be a moral wretch to disagree with. Of course she believes this! Were you to seriously raise this question in conversation, she might well be offended by the mere suggestion that it should be treated as an open question. But you need spend only half a day with Lucille to see that she believes no such thing at all. Her language and behavior exhibit a clear and habitual disdain for African Americans in her context. She does not believe them to be equally valuable, equally loved by God, and equally to be respected. It's not quite that she's being hypocritical or dishonest. She sincerely thinks that she believes this. But she doesn't.

How could this be? How could she be so mistaken about her beliefs? No doubt, the answer is complicated. But unquestionably it has to do, partially at least, with the social pressures in her context. As we noticed in chapter one, our social context is one in which racism has been given a promotion in the order of vices. Imagine the stomach it takes in our setting to admit to yourself and others that you *don't* believe that people of different ethnicities are equally valuable or equally to be respected. Lucille knows what "good Christian people" are supposed to believe about this, and she knows of herself that she's a good Christian person. So, of course, she believes all of these things about people of different ethnicities!

Every year, I'm given a fairly detailed statement of Biola University's doctrinal position. Each year, my continued employment is contingent upon my re-affirming belief in these various doctrines. I've got three small kids and a mortgage. Laurel, my wife, is a stay-at-home mom right now, and the job market in philosophy is atrocious. *Of course* I still believe all of this stuff! Imagine the stomach it would take to admit to myself and others that I *don't* believe these things anymore! It would mean the immediate forgoing of economic stability — not to mention a kind of alienation from a significant chunk of my social group.

Ever heard a presentation of the gospel that goes something like this? You have a sin problem. Your sin problem separates you from the God who created you. Unless your sin problem is dealt with, you will spend an eternity — starting at the moment of your physical death — in unutterable torment. Fortunately, God has made arrangements in the birth, death, and resurrection of Jesus to manage your sin problem. If you will believe that Jesus has done this work on your behalf then your sin problem will be managed. You will enjoy an eternity of indescribable bliss, rather than unutterable torment, beginning at the moment of your physical death. Sounds good? Okay! Ready? Set? Believe!

Now there's much to pick at in this presentation of the gospel and in the various forms it takes in public discourse. Most are alive to the worry, for example, that this gospel is sometimes presented in an emotionally loaded environment conducive to less-than-fully-reflective decision making. The result, one might worry, is belief based on fleeting emotion rather than sound thinking. Fewer, though, are fully alive to the possibility that this presentation of the gospel, whether in an emotionally charged setting or not, is a recipe for self-deception.

Suppose I believe what the evangelist is telling me, either because I think the arguments are good or because I'm swept up in the emotion of the moment — for the purposes of this argument, it doesn't really matter which. I'm suddenly faced with the following choice: (1) believe and secure an eternal life of bliss with God or (2) don't believe and risk eternal torment.

Sometimes I offer my students a thousand dollars if they'll simply believe that there is a pink elephant standing next to me at the lectern. I even give them a few minutes with eyes closed and heads bowed to work up the relevant belief. I have yet to have anyone take the deal. They know that nobody will believe them if they claim to have taken on the belief, so they chuckle at the ridiculous invitation. We all know that belief just doesn't work that way.

Interestingly, though, we seem to forget that belief doesn't work that way when we go out evangelizing. We present our friends with the rewards and punishments associated with believing, or failing to believe, that Jesus died for their sins and conquered death in his resurrection. We then invite them to bow their heads and take on the belief. When they open their eyes, we invite them to think of themselves as believers — as having crossed over from non-belief to belief.

It won't be long before they'll be aware of a certain tension between their lived experience and what they think of themselves as believing. "Why," one might ask, "do I not naturally *act* as though Jesus gave his life for me? Why don't I find myself behaving toward him the way I would toward any other living human being who suffered what he suffered to set me free?" So long as we take it for granted that we believe — after all, isn't that what happened at conversion? — we'll assume that the problem is behavioral. "I'm just having the hardest time acting out my beliefs," we'll say.

But with very few exceptions, no one has any trouble acting out their beliefs. You *do* act in accordance with your beliefs. More likely, you just don't believe what you've thought of yourself as believing. Rather than trying to work up behavior consistent with what we think we believe, we should be begging with the man who wanted desperately for Jesus to free his son from the demon that possessed him, "I believe; help my unbelief!" (Mark 9:24).

What Is Self-Deception?

So the possibility of self-deception rears its head whenever there is a kind of felt pressure associated with believing something. A mother can't live with the belief that her child is on drugs. A husband can't live with the belief that his wife is cheating. A new convert can't live with the belief that he's going to hell for lack of belief. We'll explore additional conditions that give rise to self-deception in the chapters to come. Before we do, though, it's worth pausing to attempt a more precise description of the phenomenon in question. What exactly is self-deception?

One helpful way to begin is by reflecting on the nature of deception more generally. Interpersonal deception is everywhere, and we're likely to make some headway toward an understanding of self-deception by reflecting on the conditions under which we would say that interpersonal deception has occurred.

Consider a run-of-the-mill instance of interpersonal deceit. George asks Ben where Nancy is. Ben knows that Nancy is at her house. But it's important to Ben that George stay away from the house for a while, and he knows that George will go to the house straightaway if he's honest about Nancy's whereabouts. So he tells George that Nancy's out shopping. She should be home in an hour or so. George believes Ben and heads to the local coffee shop to bide the time until Nancy's expected arrival at home.

Unquestionably, George has been deceived by Ben. George now has a false belief about Nancy's whereabouts. He came to that false belief because Ben intentionally misled him — in this case, by lying to him.

Notice, though, that Ben need not have actually lied in order to deceive George. Suppose George had asked Ben whether or not Nancy was at home. Suppose Ben, knowing that Nancy's car is parked in the closed garage, answers with a question: "Did you see her car in the driveway when we drove past?" George remembers seeing an empty driveway and concludes that Nancy is not at home. In this case, Ben doesn't lie. He simply asks a question with the intention of leading George to a hasty conclusion. If he knows Nancy's car is in the garage and intends to mislead George with his question, we say he's deceiving George even though he never lies. Overt lying is not essential for deception.

On the other hand, the *intention* to mislead *is* essential. If Ben actually believes Nancy to be shopping, he doesn't deceive George when he tells him that she's shopping, even if what he says is false. If I believe that I'm leading you to the truth with what I'm saying, I'm not deceiving you — even if I am causing you to have a false belief. In acts of deception, the deceiver typically acts for the sake of leading the deceived away from what he, the deceiver, takes to be the truth.

But it's only what the deceiver *takes to be the truth* that matters. Suppose Nancy really is out shopping. Ben thinks she's at home but doesn't want George to think she's at home, so he makes up a story to the effect that she's out shopping. In this case, Ben can be rightly counted as deceiving George. He's acting for the sake of leading George away from what he takes to be the truth. In this case, the deception misfires. In spite of himself, he causes George to believe what's true — that Nancy is out shopping. So believing what is false is not essential to having been a victim of deception. One might fall prey to deception and nevertheless believe what's true — perhaps by sheer luck! That George believes what is true is no reason to think that he's not been totally taken in by Ben's intention to deceive him.

Notice, finally, that it's not always wrong to deceive. Perhaps the reason Ben is trying to keep George away from the house is so that Nancy can put the final touches on George's surprise birthday party. Ben later brags about the skill with which he deceived George. The party was a success in part because of the success of his deception. Most think Ben hasn't done anything wrong. The deception in this case is morally acceptable. In a similar but more serious case, most think it morally acceptable to deceive a murderer as to the location of his would-be victim. While we value truth-telling, there are other things we value more highly.

Notice that deception can occur even if the deceiver has no idea what the truth is. Suppose Ben doesn't know where Nancy is. He knows that the surprise party for George starts in an hour at Nancy's house. She might be at her house making last-minute preparations, or she might be out doing last-minute shopping. He knows that if George believes Nancy's at home, he'll go there straightaway. So he tells George that she's out shopping. Ben deceives George. But in this case, he doesn't deceive him by leading him away from what he takes to be the truth. He doesn't have an opinion about what's true in this case. Rather, he's intentionally manipulating George's belief *without regard for truth*. Ben doesn't really care whether or not George believes what's true. All that matters to Ben is that George believe that Nancy is not at home.

Notice finally that deception can occur even when the deceived already has the belief in question. Suppose George already believes that Nancy's out shopping. But it suddenly occurs to him that she's left her wallet with him. He suggests to Ben that they stop at the mall, find Nancy, and give Nancy her wallet. Always quick on his feet, Ben convinces George that they'd never find her in the mall and that she'll be able to borrow money from Sue, with whom she's shopping. By putting down the plan to find Nancy in the mall, Ben acts for the purpose of protecting George's already existing belief that Nancy's at the mall. He doesn't cause George to have a new belief, and he may not have said anything that isn't true. But he puts down a plan that might have caused an undesirable *change* of belief. And the reason the change would have been undesirable is that it would have spoiled the surprise party. More to the point, Ben is acting for the sake of managing George's beliefs but is *not* acting for the sake of helping George's beliefs along toward accuracy.

So I am counted as deceiving you if I act for the sake of causing you to believe something, or to continue to believe something, without regard for the truth. I'm trying to manage your beliefs, but I'm not trying to move you along toward *true* belief.

In self-deception, I am both the deceived and the deceiver. I am deceiving myself if I'm managing my beliefs with no regard for the truth. I'm trying to manage my beliefs, but I'm not trying to move myself along toward *true* belief.

The points we've just made about interpersonal deception are equally applicable in the case of self-deception. I may deceive myself by telling an explicit lie. I may lie about a painful event in my diary, for example, hoping that memory will fade over time and I'll come to believe what I've written. But self-deception needn't involve overt lying. In fact, many of the most effective strategies for self-deception do not involve overt lying. Chapters three and four explore some of these strategies.

Things are slightly complicated, though, by the fact that I'm not deceiving myself every time I cause myself to have a false belief. I rush to get my checkbook balanced in order to get to my daughter's ballet lesson. In my rush, I make a mistake. It's my fault. Nobody caused me to rush and to have the resulting false belief about my bank balance. Still, we don't think of this as a case of self-deception. It's just a mistake. In self-deception, there is an attempt to manage belief for some reason *other* than the pursuit of truth. My math error was made in the pursuit of truth (rushed as it might have been), not in the pursuit of some other aim.

Self-deception can facilitate not only the acquisition of new beliefs, but also the retention of old ones. I came to believe the gospel because my parents told me it was true. I trusted them on the topic, and self-deception played no role in the acquisition of the belief. Still, the retention of that belief could be a result of self-deceptive strategies. Remember that one can be deceived into believing something true. Likewise, one can be self-deceived in believing something that is in fact true. Whether or not one is deceived (in the present sense) has to do with how one comes to have or retain the belief — not with whether or not the belief is true.

One can be self-deceived about any number of things. A common topic of self-deception is, not surprisingly, oneself. I care deeply about myself. Beliefs about myself are often emotionally laden. Unlike my beliefs about the planet Jupiter, for example, my beliefs about myself are beliefs that, when considered, evoke strong emotions.

But to be self-deceived is not simply to be deceived about oneself. Any subject that evokes strong emotion is a good candidate for self-deception. For example, some Christians hold their eschatological beliefs — beliefs about how the end times will unfold — about as loosely as I hold my beliefs about Jupiter. They're unlikely to be self-deceived about the end times. But for others, eschatology is a matter of passionate debate. These folks ought to be more watchful in this area for the signs of self-deception.

So much for an initial characterization of self-deception. As we've seen, it occurs whenever we manage our own beliefs without an eye on making progress toward the truth. It is most likely to occur when we have strong emotional attachments to belief on some topic. When we have no attachments, the general desire to believe what's true is likely to guide our inquiry.

Jean-Paul Sartre's characterization of self-deception is, perhaps, the most concise and helpful for our purposes. According to Sartre, to be self-deceived is to avoid using rational standards for evidence whenever it suits our purposes.

Truth and rationality aren't the only things we value, of course, and often the other things we value influence our inquiry in such a way as to make believing what's true less likely. We will leave it an open question, at this point, whether or not this is an acceptable condition. Should we care about truth above all else? For now, it's worth noting that when it comes to the management of another person's belief, we allow some things to trump the truth — for example, preventing a horrific crime. We think it allowable, and probably even a very good idea, to lie if in so doing we can keep someone from getting killed.

The chapters to come explain in some detail what self-deceptive strategies might look like for Christians. Once we've seen how self-deception shows up in our lived experience, we'll be better positioned to ask what we should do about it.

CHAPTER 3

How-To, Part 1:
Attention Management
and Procrastination

S UPPOSE I'VE AGREED, CONSCIOUSLY or otherwise, to take the deal. Whether or not I know it, I'm ready to take up a belief for reasons having nothing to do with the strength of evidence available to me in support of that belief. How do I do it? In the first chapter, we marveled at the fact that people do, in fact, manage to deceive themselves. But how? How can we manage to be both the deceiver and the deceived? How do we not catch ourselves in the act? Obviously, we'll need to employ some sort of strategy. And the more compelling our evidence *against* the belief in question, the more subtlety will be required in the strategy employed. In this and the next chapter, we will explore some of the common strategies for taking the deal without catching yourself in the act.

On one level, the capacity for self-deception is not at all puzzling.

I am not a morning person. The simple act of getting out of bed to start the day is often for me a Herculean task. Over the years, I've employed countless self-deceptive and self-manipulative strategies to avoid missing morning classes. I set the coffee machine for fifteen minutes before my scheduled wake-up time, so that my first thought after the alarm goes off will be of the fresh coffee waiting for me — if only I can make it to the kitchen. I promise myself a mid-afternoon nap as a reward for getting up *now* and, although I've rarely made good on the promise, I believe in the moment that *this time* I *really* mean it. I put the alarm on the other side of the room so that I'll have to get out of bed to turn it off — or at least I'll have to get out of bed each time I hit the snooze button. I set the time on my alarm clock thirty minutes ahead of the actual time to induce short-term panic at the moment of waking.

In at least two of these self-manipulative strategies, I am both the deceiver and the deceived. In the one strategy, I convince myself that, though I virtually never make good on the promise to take an afternoon nap, I will *this time*. And in the other, I convince myself that it's thirty minutes later than it is.

When I set the time on my alarm thirty minutes ahead, I avail myself of an anticipated blind spot in my thought life. I'm betting on the fact that my belief about the time will come fairly immediately upon seeing the alarm clock — that the resulting panic will set in *before* memory gets going and I recall setting the clock ahead. When I promise myself a mid-afternoon nap, I direct all of my attention to the schedule for the day ahead in order to find the perfect little gap for forty winks. I assiduously avoid any thought of the past. In particular, I avoid any thought of past occasions on which I broke this promise to myself.

In this case, the self-deception comes easy. It comes easy, in part, because the false belief needn't last long in order to accomplish its purpose. It's okay if, ten minutes into my morning routine, I remember that it's thirty minutes earlier than I think it is. By that time, I'm out of bed and on my way. Similarly, it usually dawns on me fairly early in the day that I won't be taking the nap

I promised myself. But that's okay, too. The lie did its work, and I'm out of bed and on my way.

On the other hand, in the really interesting cases, I need not only to acquire, but also to *persist in,* the false belief. I need to deceive myself in such a way as to conceal the lie over the long haul. I'll need to be more subtle in my strategy. So what are these more subtle strategies? And where do they show up in Christian experience?

Attention Management

In *The Violent Bear It Away,* Flannery O'Connor's Tarwater is a man busy about the task of suppressing his knowledge of Christ. O'Connor's description of Tarwater's inner life is worth quoting at length:

> In the darkest, most private part of his soul, hanging upside down like a sleeping bat, was the certain undeniable knowledge that he was not hungry for the bread of life. Had the bush flamed for Moses, the sun stood still for Joshua, the lions turned aside before Daniel only to prophesy the bread of life? Jesus? He felt a terrible disappointment in that conclusion, a dread that it was true. . . . He tried when possible to pass over these thoughts, to keep his vision located on an even level, to see no more than what was in front of his face and to let his eyes stop at the surface of that. It was as if he were afraid that if he let his eye rest for an instant longer than was needed to place something — a spade, a hoe, the mule's hind quarters before his plow, the red furrow under him — that the thing would suddenly stand before him, strange and terrifying,

demanding that he name it and name it justly and be judged for the name he gave it. He did all he could to avoid this threatened intimacy of creation.[1]

William James said that "my experience is what I agree to attend to. Only those items I notice shape my mind." The most common strategies for long-haul self-deception involve the management of attention. Through habitual and systematic management of my cognitive gaze, I can come to believe things that I wouldn't believe were I to attend indiscriminately to my surroundings. Through attention management, I exercise a degree of control over what comes into my mind. And this, in turn, affects what I believe.

I first came to the study of philosophy through an interest in apologetics. I found philosophically trained Christian apologists handling with some care the difficult questions that others in my Christian context seemed to gloss over. Is there good evidence for God's existence, for the reliability of the Scriptures, or for the historical resurrection of Jesus? Can the reality of evil be squared with the existence of the Christian God? I read books on these and other topics by Christian apologists. I found the evidence supporting the truth of orthodox Christianity impressive, and that was a source of great comfort and increased faith.

Before long, though, I also noticed that the people most impressed by the arguments favoring orthodox Christianity were the orthodox Christians. Now this in itself isn't at all surprising. I suppose the people most impressed by the arguments for *anything* will be the people who believe in that thing, whatever it is. The

1. Flannery O'Connor, *The Violent Bear It Away*, in *Three* (New York: Signet Books, 1964), p. 136. Thanks to Jason Baehr for calling my attention to this passage.

people most impressed by the evidence for extra-terrestrial life, for example, will tend to be the people who believe in extra-terrestrial life. Arguably, it's *because* they've found the evidence compelling that they now believe what they do. So a correlation between people who find the evidence for Christianity compelling and people who believe that Christianity is true is not surprising.

What struck me, though, was the seeming infrequency of a *change of mind* in either direction upon initial confrontation with the evidence. Christians I knew who carefully considered the evidence for the first time tended to find it impressive. Non-Christians I knew who carefully considered the evidence for the first time tended to find it wanting. And if they didn't, they'd likely fault the person articulating their side of the issue for a less-than-adequate presentation of the evidence. I've found it almost as unlikely that people will change their minds about Christianity at a debate as it is that they will change their sports loyalties after seeing their favorite team lose.

But how do we do this? How do Christians manage to find the same body of evidence supportive of Christianity that non-Christians find to discredit Christianity? How do Christians and non-Christians alike manage to remain unimpressed by the evidence against their position? The answer, in part, is that we do this by managing our attention. To a significant degree, we control the character of our experience by deciding what to attend to. Those experiences, in turn, result in our having the beliefs that we do.

When the movie *The Da Vinci Code* hit the theaters and the swirl of related controversy began to pick up speed, I decided finally to read the book so that I wouldn't be found ignorant at dinner parties. I went to the bookstore on campus at a prominent conservative Christian university in my area. I quickly located five different books by Christian authors criticizing Dan Brown's work. But I searched in vain for the book itself. Finally, I went to the sales desk for help. I was politely informed by the nineteen-year-old student worker behind the counter that there were no copies in stock. I asked if they were temporarily sold out. Could I place one on order?

"No," he said with a slightly holier-than-thou tone, "we don't carry that book."

"But you do carry five books criticizing that book?" I asked.

"Yep."

"You don't find that odd?"

"Nope."

"What kind of inquiry do you suppose this ordering policy recommends?"

We stared blankly at each other — or maybe past each other — for a second or two, and then he turned his attention to the next customer in line.

Not long ago I visited a friend who said that he had recently been convicted about the fact that he'd not really "checked into the veracity" of his Christian beliefs. So he had recently made it something of a project to look into the evidence for and against the Christian tradition into which he'd been born and raised. He wanted to take a step back and see whether or not the stuff he'd been raised with was actually true. I asked him what he'd been reading. He pointed me to a collection of about eight to ten books on the evidence for and against Christian belief on his shelf — not bad for a busy professional with a young family. But upon closer examination, I noticed that all of the books had Christian authors.

"These books are all written by Christians," I pointed out.

"Yep. I've been making apologetics a sort of hobby. I especially like the stuff by Craig, Strobel, and Geisler."

"Do you suppose there are non-Christians writing on this topic?"

"I suppose there probably are."

"Do you know who they are?"

"No. I haven't really looked for that sort of thing."

Now I don't mean to suggest that what my friend was doing is a bad idea. There's nothing wrong with trying to shore up your faith with evidence. There's a wealth of very good material out there on the rationality of Christian belief, and Christians do themselves a favor by getting acquainted with it. But to think of this as a genuine checking into the veracity of Christian belief is a bit of a stretch. It's a bit like checking into the claims of "holistic medicine" by reading only those studies written by its practitioners and ignoring the critical treatment of these practices in "mainstream" medical journals.

The belief that Christianity is well supported by the evidence, or at least is not ruled out as irrational by the evidence, is a source of great comfort for me. It's also a source of great comfort for me to know that I've taken a more-or-less careful and objective look at the evidence for and against Christian claims. But an honest-to-goodness inquiry into the evidence for and against Christian belief is hard — not to mention risky and scary — work. If it turned out that Christianity were irrational, I'd be faced with a tough choice: either settle into a commitment to an irrational religion, or suspend my belief in the truth of Christianity and suffer considerable social consequences (including the loss of my job and alienation from my closest friends and family, as I mentioned before).

So life offers me a deal. Believe that Christianity is rational whether or not the evidence available to me suggests that it is. Believe further that, at least for a season, I "took a step back" and looked into the evidence for and against Christian claims.

But how can I bring myself to believe these things without catching myself in the act? One strategy is to conduct my inquiry in such a way as to systematically attend to evidence likely to support Christian belief and assiduously avoid evidence in the other direction. Over time, if I'm only or even primarily exposed to the evidence as presented by those with Christian sympathies, I may well find myself believing that Christianity is true, or I may find it easier to retain my belief if I'm already a Christian. One strategy, then, for acquiring and retaining beliefs that contribute to your own felt well-being is to attend exclusively or primarily to the evidence as presented by those sympathetic with the desired belief.

Arguably, plenty of people who think of themselves as "checking into the truth of Christian claims" have taken the deal. And it's not that they're doing something that isn't worth doing. Again, it's not a bad idea to bolster one's faith with reasons. Lots of people have been greatly helped by a careful study of the evidence — as presented by Christians — for the truth of Christianity. It's rather that they're not doing what they've told themselves they're doing. They're not conducting anything like an objective inquiry into the truth-value of Christian claims. But it's the belief that they *are* conducting a more-or-less objective inquiry which is the source of such great comfort for them.

The strategy shows up not only where the truth of Christianity is concerned, but also *within* the context of Christian belief wherever the emotional stakes for believing are high. The homosexual

Christian finds himself reading with greater concentration and interest those authors who argue that there is nothing immoral or non-biblical about monogamous homosexual lifestyles, while his opponent finds himself reading with greater concentration and interest those authors who argue that homosexuality is immoral and contrary to biblical ethical standards. The woman who discerns in herself the gift of preaching reads with greater concentration and interest those authors who defend egalitarian interpretations of the relevant biblical passages. The man who considers himself a prophet finds himself attending to evidence for "continuationism" — the view that the full range of spiritual gifts are in play today — while the woman who's seen self-proclaimed prophets do considerable harm attends more carefully to the evidence for "cessationism" — the view that the supernatural gifts ceased after the apostolic age. Wherever there is disagreement and people are significantly emotionally attached to one side or the other, the conditions are right for attention management of this sort.

Interestingly, though, attention management sometimes works in the opposite direction. So far, we've been examining the tendency to direct attention toward evidence *for* favorable beliefs, one in which evidence in the other direction is avoided. Sometimes, though, we pay inordinate attention to the evidence *against* our view in order to discredit that evidence.

In one fascinating study some years ago, subjects were presented with evidence suggesting that there was a correlation between heavy caffeine use and breast cancer. Subjects were then asked to report on whether or not (or to what degree) they found the evidence convincing. In the female population, heavy consumers of caffeine were significantly less convinced than were those who consumed less. The male population was significantly more convinced than were the female heavy consumers, and there was little difference between heavy and light caffeine consumers in the male population. The studies revealed, in other words, that those for whom the hypothesis was bad news were least likely to be convinced by the evidence.

Related studies reveal that we often spend more time scrutinizing evidence for a view if we find it threatening than if we find it benign. This is especially true if we're presented with the evidence in public. Apparently, we're more likely to scrutinize evidence for opposing views if we think we'll be called on to answer for that evidence. If we believe we've been presented with the evidence in private, we're less likely to give it much attention.[2]

If you live and move in a typical Protestant Christian environment, try this experiment. In a visible location somewhere in your house (the refrigerator, say, or on the calendar by your phone) display the text of Ephesians 2:8-9:

> For by grace you have been saved through faith, and this is not
> your own doing; it is the gift of God — not the result of works,
> so that no one may boast.

Go ahead and rip it right out of context and put it in clear view. In another equally visible location, put James 2:24 on display:

> You see that a person is justified by works and not by faith alone.

2. See Z. Kunda, "Motivated Inference: Self-Serving Generation and Evaluation of Causal Theories," *Journal of Personality and Social Psychology* 53 (1987): 636-47, as well as Baumeister and Cairns, "Repression and Self-Presentation: When Audiences Interfere with Self-Deceptive Strategies," *Journal of Personality and Social Psychology* 62 (1992): 851-62, for more detailed description of these studies.

Once again, go ahead and rip it right out of context and put it in clear view. Leave these two quotes in place for several weeks, and see which of the two gets more attention. My money is on James. Confronted with this seeming anomaly, your Protestant friends will want to attend more closely to the James passage. What's the context? Maybe we should consult a few commentaries. Perhaps a word study or two is in order. What does James mean by "justified"? What does he mean by "works"? Interestingly, the Ephesians passage won't receive anything like this kind of careful scrutiny.

One of the most interesting things to learn about any Christian community is *which* passages they allow themselves to quote out of context. Most Protestants are perfectly happy to recite Ephesians 2:8-9 without any nuance or contextual explanation. Not so with James 2:24. On its face, the James passage is an unwelcome affront to good Protestant doctrine, according to which we are justified by grace alone through faith alone. So we give it our attention. We scrutinize. We discredit it (you've just got to love Martin Luther for writing James out of the canon) or we explain it away.

Attention management, then, has two sides. On the one hand, we manage to deceive ourselves by systematically avoiding attention to evidence against those beliefs upon which our felt well-being depends. On the other hand, we direct inordinate *critical* attention to evidence that opposes our cherished belief if that evidence can't be avoided or if we think we'll have to answer for it in public. We give it our attention, it seems, not so much to learn from it as to creatively discount it. Either way, through careful management of attention, we enable ourselves to be deceived over the long haul. Attention management, then, is the first of our self-deceptive strategies.

Goleman sums it up nicely in the form of one of R. D. Laing's "knots."

> The range of what we think and do
> Is limited by what we fail to notice
> And because we fail to notice
> *That* we fail to notice
> There is little we can do
> To change
> Until we notice
> How failing to notice
> Shapes our thoughts and deeds.[3]

Procrastination

In *The Sickness unto Death,* Kierkegaard describes a "moment" familiar to all of us. It is the "little tiny transition from having understood to doing." Here's what he says about it:

> . . . if a person does not do what is right the very second he knows it is the right thing to do — then, for a start, the knowledge comes off the boil. Next comes the question of what the will thinks of the knowledge. The will is dialectical and has underneath it the whole of man's lower nature. If it doesn't like the knowledge, it doesn't immediately follow that the will goes and does the op-

---

3. Daniel Goleman, *Vital Lies, Simple Truths: The Psychology of Self-Deception* (New York: Simon and Schuster, 1985), p. 24.

posite of what was grasped in knowing — such strong contrasts are presumably rare; but then the will lets some time pass; there is an interim called "We'll look into it tomorrow." During all this the knowing becomes more and more obscured, and the lower nature more and more victorious.... And then when the knowing has become duly obscured, the will and the knowing can better understand one another. Eventually they are in entire agreement, since knowing has now deserted to the side of the will and allows it to be known that what the will wants is quite right.[4]

Beliefs are sometimes demanding. Often they break in on us unexpectedly and take to ordering us around like uninvited tyrants. One minute we're sailing happily through life. The next minute, we find ourselves with an uncomfortably demanding belief. This tyrant takes office and issues an imperative with such compelling force that we're unable to look him in the eye and say "no." The tyrant's authority (the seemingly obvious truth of the belief) rings through with such piercing clarity as to rule out the very thought of direct quarrel. Nothing other than unquestioned obedience can be seriously entertained. While the tyrant will have nothing of direct defiance, though, he can often be appeased by the promise of *deferred* obedience. If we promise him obedience later, he'll often take the bait. And if we put him off long enough, he might just go away.

She's been in hard labor for fifteen hours and she's only dilated two centimeters. She's exhausted, discouraged, and in

---

4. Søren Kierkegaard, *Sickness unto Death* (New York: Penguin Classics, 1989), pp. 126-27. For a nice discussion of this and other passages in Kierkegaard, see Mike Martin, *Self-Deception and Morality* (Lawrence: University Press of Kansas, 1986), pp. 58ff.

terrible pain. The lights are too bright, the nurse on duty is not sufficiently responsive, and her husband — bless him for trying so hard — reeks of onion rings. She'd lose her stomach if there were anything in it to lose. She's starving, but the very thought of eating is insufferable. She's dying of thirst — and they're feeding her ice chips. *Ice chips!* The tyrant takes office. She finds herself with the belief that no rational person would do this voluntarily *twice*. She will never do this again. She *must* never do this again. She must *promise* never to do this again.

But she always thought they'd have more than one — at least two, maybe three. She stops short of promising herself never to have another child. But neither can she defy the tyrant. She's in no position to resist the piercing clarity of his claim. This *is* unbearable, and she can't bring herself to insist on her plans for multiple children. So she puts him off. She'll take up this question again . . . later.

We all know — and all but first-born children among us are thankful for — what happens next. Slowly, the belief that childbirth is unbearable fades into obscurity — along with its categorical demand never to go in for it again. It wasn't *really* unbearable. After all, I made it. And look at my beautiful baby girl! It's a reasonable trade-off — that pain for the miracle in my arms.

The tyrant is gone.

"These images seem a little PG-13 for a church service," he thinks, as he half deflects his gaze from the screen. The multimedia presentation unveils the lives of children in the inner city, abandoned or living under the "care" of drug-addicted, homeless parents. This particular slide presents a young girl (is she even a teenager?) with a muddy face sitting in what looks like a gutter. The voice behind the image says that she was selling drugs (and worse) to support herself and her younger siblings. After about ten minutes, the multimedia presentation ends, mercifully, and a couple in their forties takes the stage. They say these children are everywhere. We drive past them every time we're anywhere near the city. "I drove back and forth to school through a neighborhood like that for four years," he thinks. "How is it that I don't remember seeing anything like *that?*" The woman is talking about the fact that these children are the forgotten ones. She explains with tears in her eyes how she and her husband have abandoned "normal life" in order to be Christ for these abandoned children. Whatever time is not spent embracing, feeding, loving, and providing health care for these children is spent in front of church congregations like this one. They invite the congregation to pray for them. It's a sincere invitation. But everyone knows they need our money.

Pastor Doug takes the stage and leads the congregation in a prayer for this amazing couple. He then explains that any money placed in the white envelope in the bulletin will go directly to this ministry. As he so often does with such passion, grace, and humility, Pastor Doug exhorts the congregation to stretch out in generosity toward these dear folks who've given up everything for the sake of what James calls "pure and undefiled religion" (James 1:27).

He believes — he *knows* — that Pastor Doug is right. This really is pure and undefiled religion at its best. He thinks of the extravagance of his life, of his kids' lives, in comparison with these lost children. His kids have so much *stuff!* There are twice as many bikes in his garage as there are people in his family. He believes that this cause is just. He believes that this couple is sincere. He believes that he has more than enough money to contribute generously to the cause. He believes it would be a moral outrage to say "no" to this request from his financial position. He believes that he should put a hundred dollars in the white envelope. Why that number? He's not sure. But he knows beyond a shadow of a doubt that he should give that amount.

The tyrant has taken office. These beliefs are demanding. They present themselves with such clarity that he'd have to forsake his very humanity to deny them. What kind of a wretch would he be to say no? He can't take seriously anything other than the intention to give to this cause.

But he stops short of actual obedience. He doesn't have the cash. He could write a check. But didn't his wife just purchase an airline ticket out of that account? Does it have the hundred dollars in it? If he overdraws his account, there's a hefty fee. Then again, maybe there's more in the account than he thinks! Maybe he can give *more* than a hundred dollars! He'll get online after church and take a look at his finances. Once he's got a better grasp of his financial situation, he'll give to this cause. He picks up the prayer card on his way out of the service so he'll know where to send the money.

Next thing he knows, it's Wednesday. Driving to school for a meeting, he remembers the presentation at church. Somehow, the beliefs don't present themselves as forcefully now. It's a good cause, of course. But there are millions of good causes. He's not a stingy person. He's given (and he's currently giving) to plenty of good causes. Still, he'll give to this cause. When he gets home tonight, he'll find that prayer card, write a check, and send it to this ministry.

His next conscious thought of the ministry occurs about a year later. He's writing a book on self-deception and he's searching his memory for illustrations of self-deception by means of procrastination. Interestingly, he's not wracked with guilt over not having given. He should have given, to be sure. But he's not a moral wretch for not having given. Certainly he's not been inhumane. A little careless, maybe, but not inhumane.

The tyrant is gone.

Often our strongest moral beliefs (beliefs to the effect that we *ought* to do this or *ought not* do that) will diminish or even disappear if we procrastinate acting on them. So whenever a moral belief moves in and demands uncomfortable action, life offers us the deal. Agree to act on this moral belief . . . but not now. Agree with yourself to act upon it *later*. Often, procrastination will cause the belief to wane in strength. And if you can put off action long enough, the belief might disappear altogether.

In some circles, procrastination has found its way into something like received doctrine. An honest and straightforward reading of the New Testament makes it as plain as anything that the disciples of Jesus experienced radical character transformation as a result of having taken up Christ as master. They recorded Jesus as having called his followers to perfect obedience to the Law of God. They wrote that Christians would be judged according to their deeds. And they exhorted one another to move further into the abundant life of Jesus — to put off the lives of sin and selfishness out of which they had been called and to put on a new life of humility, peace, patience, and joyful service to others. In all of this, they were writing and speaking out of the abundance of their experience. Presumably, they had experienced noticeable and significant progress toward Christ-likeness. This is why they had no reservations about calling others to it as well.

So we find ourselves with the belief that we too (insofar as we consider ourselves Christians) should find our way into radical character transformation toward Christ-likeness. This belief comes so compellingly to us from the pages of the New Testament that direct defiance is unthinkable. We can't bring ourselves to say in one and the same breath, "I'm a Christian, but I have no intention of putting on the heart and character of Christ." We can't bring ourselves to say that we have no intention to make significant and noticeable progress toward Christ-likeness.

But neither do we find ourselves simply doing the things of Jesus. Perhaps we can't find a single observable respect in which we are more Christ-like now than we were five years ago. Nearly all Christians will tell you that they have every intention of being perfected. The only real disagreement has to do with *when* we will make significant and noticeable progress toward perfection.

Many have agreed to take on the heart of Jesus, but they're planning to do it later . . . *much later.* They'll have the character of Jesus — just not now. For now, they'll be, as the bumper sticker says, "not perfect . . . just forgiven." Having received forgiveness because of the work of Jesus on the cross, they'll live with the expectation that perfection will come to them all at once in the blink of an eye at the moment of passing from this life to the next. As a result, they procrastinate acting upon the clear biblical imperative to put on perfection. And the longer they procrastinate, the less clear it is to them that this is really what they ought to be doing anyway.

At this point, procrastination joins forces with attention management. It's extremely difficult to reconcile with the witness of Scripture the belief that noticeable progress toward Christ-likeness awaits my bodily death. So I'll need to direct my attention to those passages that emphasize themes like grace, forgiveness, and passivity. I'll need either to avoid attention to, or explain away, those passages suggesting that I'm expected to work hard *now* to make progress toward Christ-likeness *in this life*. It'll help if I can find a church where the pastor regularly reminds his flock that he's no further along toward holiness than are any of the parishioners in his care. After all, any suggestion to the effect that someone *else* has made significant and noticeable progress toward Christ-likeness puts me at risk of expecting such progress myself.

By means of procrastination and attention management, then, we find our way *out* of the pursuit of perfection which characterizes the great ones in the way of Jesus Christ. We convince ourselves that perfection isn't the goal — isn't it impossible anyway? — and that we've got no business taking it seriously or chasing after it, at least not in *this* life. We certainly shouldn't have the audacity to exhort others in its direction. And the predictable result is a church full of Christians whose lives are indistinguishable (or worse) from the lives of their non-Christian co-workers. After all, they're *just forgiven,* and *being forgiven* doesn't have any observable connection to lifestyle or the condition of one's heart. You can be perfectly forgiven and a perfect wretch.

So here are two prominent strategies for taking the deal: attention management and procrastination. Before we're done, we'll want to ask whether or not these abilities of ours are to be lamented or celebrated. Presumably God could have created us in such a way that we always attend indiscriminately to our surroundings and act immediately upon our clear moral convictions. But he didn't. Why? We'll also want to explore possibilities for detecting and avoiding these self-deceptive strategies wherever they derail us in our pursuit of Christ and his way. But first let's examine a few more self-deceptive strategies.

CHAPTER 4

How-To, Part 2: Perspective Switching, Rationalization, and Ressentiment

Perspective Switching

O NE OF THE MOST interesting things about the story of David and Bathsheba is that, until he was confronted by Nathan, there is no indication that David was crippled with guilt in the wake of his sin. David is the very opposite of Hawthorne's Arthur Dimmesdale, who continually invents new tortures for himself in an effort to achieve atonement for his secret sin of adultery with Hester Prynne. Not David. He seems to have carried on with life undaunted by the horror of his offense until squarely confronted with his sin by the prophet Nathan. In his tenth sermon, Bishop Joseph Butler is dismayed by the fact that "near a year must have passed, between the time of the commission of [David's] crimes and the time of the prophet's coming to him; and it does not appear from the story, that he had in all this while the least remorse or contrition." One wonders how a man who walked so closely with the Lord could have committed such acts of atrocity without suffering debilitating guilt.

Three years ago, I began construction on an 800-square-foot addition to my 900-square-foot house. I had intended to hire a general contractor to build the addition. But after reviewing several bids, I discovered that I would have to build the thing myself if it was to be built at all. My most ambitious home-improvement project to boast at that point had been the installation of a new garbage disposal — and I had needed a fair bit of help from a neighbor with that. So I bought books from Home Depot about plumbing and framing, solicited advice from anyone willing to give it, told my dad to clear his schedule and get his tools ready, and set to work. After a steep learning curve, several sleepless nights wondering if things were going to fall apart, and lots of un-building and re-building, we are finally living in our addition. It's glorious. And it's a source for me of what can only be described as utterly self-indulgent pride.

While I'm proud of the work, though, I'm also painfully aware of all of its defects. I know every corner that didn't come out square, every door that sticks, that there's no access to the attic to service the air conditioning ducts, and that the entire front porch is framed just slightly off level. I know where colored putty covers sloppy cuts in the wood floor and where caulk covers mitered corners that didn't come together in the crown molding.

Friends who know very little about construction swear that the addition looks like it was constructed by professionals. I like those people. Happy to have them over any time. Having them around gives me a perspective on the addition far more gratifying than my own. When I'm giving the tour to someone like this, I'm always struck anew with the splendor of my work. Any mistakes are such that no reasonable person would ever notice them. My guest doesn't notice them — so they're barely noticeable. For a little while, I'm able to see the addition as *they* see it. Life is good. My addition is a masterpiece.

Then there are the friends who know even less about construction. They couldn't tell you, even in rough terms, what's between the drywall that they see on the inside and the stucco they see on the exterior. And, as far as they know, the wood floor they're walking on sits directly on the earth below. When I give these folks the tour, they nod smilingly at what appears to be a perfectly normal house. There is nothing that even approximates appropriate appreciation for the artistry and craftsmanship involved in the production of what they're looking at. These tours are much less enjoyable for me, and they usually don't last nearly as long. I'm certainly not tempted to adopt the perspective of these ignoramuses. My own perspective (even with its recognition of mistakes here and there) is far more satisfying. When I'm with these folks, I see the addition not as they see it but as *I* see it, for the incredible accomplishment that it is, imperfections and all.

The philosopher Jean-Paul Sartre emphasized in his work the fact that we exist at all times both "for ourselves" and "for others." While we have a certain view of ourselves, we're also interested in being viewed, and in *how* we're being viewed, by others. Sartre calls our attention to the amazing capacity that we have to disregard our own view of ourselves when the view of others better serves us and to disregard the view of others when our own view is more attractive.[1]

How did David manage to live with himself after having murdered the husband of the woman with whom he had an adulterous affair? He organized things in such a way as to make available a different perspective on the events in question. David's actions

---

1. Jean-Paul Sartre, *Being and Nothingness*, trans. George J. Becker (New York: Schocken Books, 1965), p. 100.

created the appearance (for most anyway) that Uriah had died in legitimate battle. His death was tragic, of course, but not out of the ordinary. Men die in battle all the time. Bathsheba, after properly mourning, became David's wife and bore him a son. All perfectly normal. This perspective would have been shared by everyone except David, Bathsheba, and perhaps Joab. Arguably, by generating and operating from this perspective, David is able to live with himself until the prophet Nathan tricks him into focusing from his own perspective once again, at which point he is appropriately stricken with guilt.

We switch perspectives because no single perspective consistently delivers the view of things that we prefer. Perspective switching is an especially accessible form of self-deception for those in public ministry. Those who pastor, teach, disciple, or counsel others have readily available to them whatever perspective has been generated in those they serve, and the temptation will be strong to avail themselves of that perspective whenever their own perspective delivers uncomfortable views.

For Pastor Tim, the job is about more than just preaching. He's a real shepherd for his flock. He spends a great deal of time at the local Starbucks sipping chai tea and listening to his parishioners/ friends chronicle the sordid details of their twisted inner lives. One struggles with lust and confesses his struggle with discomforting detail. Another confesses to an affair about which his wife is still unaware. One can't find contentment when his friends have nicer things than he does. Another, utterly in the grip of professionalism, finds that his state of mind is completely dependent on how he's being viewed at work. It's emotionally taxing but enormously rewarding work. People regularly express deep gratitude for his genuine care and concern for the nitty-gritty of their daily walk.

And he doesn't just listen. He's also "transparent." He identifies with the man struggling with lust and reassures him with the thought that every man, himself included, struggles with "this sort of thing." He discloses to the man who struggles with professionalism that pastors regularly worry about how they're being perceived by their parishioners.

But his transparency only goes so far. Details are left out, and his parishioners are left with a view of Pastor Tim according to which he's tasted just enough of their particular vice to have a vague sense of what it must be like to have fallen as low as they have. Of course, Tim knows better. His own perspective includes the way he meticulously monitors attendance numbers each Sunday. How many chose his service over the service down the street? His own perspective includes the regular occurrence of sexual innuendo and imagery assaulting his mind even during worship and while he's preaching. His own perspective includes the acute relief from dissatisfaction he experienced when he was finally in possession of an automobile comparable in quality to his neighbors' cars. No, the perspective of his parishioners is far more appealing. From their perspective, he's transparent but still up on the pedestal — imperfect, sure, but not quite as haunted by these annoying imperfections as they may be.

But only sometimes.

Many of his parishioners are overworked and exhausted. Some of them work two jobs to support their families and, occasionally, Tim finds himself in a conversation where being overworked is the subject. Invariably, someone will make a comment about how nice it must be to sip chai tea for a living. Someone else will wink at Tim and make a comment to the effect that he'd be happy to work on Sundays if he could have the rest of the week off. This is all said tongue-in-cheek, of course. But back of it all, Tim knows, is simple ignorance about how hard it is to pastor a church. They're unaware of the complex business decisions he has to make on behalf of his congregation. They're unaware of the church-staff politics he has to mediate. They have no idea how *long* his Sunday is, how many hours of preparation go into Sunday's service during the week, how much time he spends reading and staying current in order better to serve his congregation, and how much sleep he's lost in prayer and loving concern for those with whom he sips chai tea at Starbucks. His parishioners may think of him as someone who can't identify with real hard work. But he knows better. When he finds himself in *these* conversations, his own perspective is far more appealing.

Most of us monitor with some care the perspective others have of us. Often a decision to see the world from their perspective gives us relief from painful truths that haunt us. But we're not happy to settle permanently into the perspective of the other. Our own perspective gives us special insight into our own circumstances and often yields the more attractive picture. So, as Sartre suggested, we switch back and forth depending on the demands of the moment.

Rationalization

Perspective switching is but one variation on what is perhaps the most recognizable of our strategies for self-deception: rationalization. To rationalize is to construct a rational justification for a behavior, decision, or belief arrived at in some other way. When we rationalize a behavior, for example, we locate reasons that *would* justify the behavior were they operational. We then present these reasons to ourselves and others as explaining our *actual* behavior. But the reasons are mere fictions. They play no causal role in the production of the behavior. One strategy for rationalizing, as we have seen, is to capitalize on the perspective of another. We find or create in those around us a perspective from which our actions and decisions are reasonable and right and we adopt that perspective.

Sometimes, though, there is nobody with the perspective our rationalizing requires. In this case, we are left to the devices of our imagination. We must construct — out of thin air, as it were — a story that satisfies the constraints of rationality and justifies our behavior or decision.

Remember Balaam? Balak offers him a handsome price for a simple task: curse the Israelites on behalf of God. Balaam seeks the word of the Lord on the matter and is told in no uncertain terms that God has no intention of cursing the Israelites. Balak then does what any reasonable businessman would do: he offers more money. Everyone has a price. Enticed by the new offer, Balaam checks in with God to see if perchance he's changed his mind. God doesn't give him the curse he seeks. But he gives him leave to pursue his lust for wealth. Balaam goes with Balak's men intending only to say what God gives him to say. But he hopes all the while for the opportunity to utter a divine curse on the Israelites in order to take advantage of Balak's generous offer. Balak, who thinks Balaam has agreed to come and curse the Israelites, is understandably upset when Balaam repeatedly gives a faithful report of God's blessing on the Israelites. False advertising! Finally, Balaam finds a way to satisfy the desires of his benefactor without falsely reporting the word of the Lord, which had nothing but blessing for Israel. In lieu of the elusive divine curse, he offers Balak foolproof advice for bringing down the Israelites. They can be brought down by luring them away from their God with women and food.

The Scriptures leave no doubt that Balaam was motivated by the desire for wealth to cripple the Israelites before Balak. But of course that's not the way Balaam would have told the story to himself and others. He was presented with a request. He had no intention of violating his responsibility to faithfully report the word of the Lord. But if he could satisfy the request without misrepresenting God, why not? To be sure, God had said "no" to his first request, but there can't be any harm in asking again, right? And he didn't *force* the Israelites to violate God's holiness commands. They slept with those women and ate that food of their own accord. He was simply a conduit of information. Isn't that his job as a prophet? He never misrepresented God and, one might imagine, he simply answered Balak's questions about God's relationship with the Israelites as honestly as possible. What Balak would do with that information is none of his concern. And it's certainly not his fault that the Israelites were so weak as to fall for the trap.

Not long ago, just before the subprime debacle in 2007, Dave was given the opportunity to pursue a lucrative career as a mortgage broker. To be competitive in the business, though, he would be required to present potential clients with the opportunity to lie about their income on their loan applications. When he asked around, Christians in the mortgage business told Dave that there would be nothing at all wrong with his selling these loans. His job would simply be to present the potential client with the options. What they did with those options would be none of his concern. In any case, it was explained, the banks know what they're doing with these stated-income loans. It's not *really* a lie if the person you're giving false information to (in this case, the bank) is *inviting* the false information — if it's a win/win on both sides of the lie. Think of all the people he'll be helping into home ownership who might be incapable of securing a home otherwise? Furthermore, there really are a lot of truly dangerous loans out there. Dave could be a force for good in an otherwise corrupt industry by looking out for the best interest of his clients. They may need to lie about their income to get the loan he'd sell them — and he may have to knowingly sign fraudulent loan applications — but he wouldn't be one of these brokers guiding people into the *truly* dangerous loans just to make a higher commission.

To his credit, Dave could never get past the idea that he would have to sign his name to loan applications he would know to be falsified. He spent a fair bit of time and energy trying to figure out whether or not he could be competitive without selling these loans. Eventually he turned down the opportunity.

Christians in the loan business at that time found themselves in a tough spot — one in which making a profit and surviving in business seemed to require behavior that was morally gray at best. So they muddled through as best they could. But few of them would accept a description of things according to which they had chosen morally questionable activity for the sake of profit and survival in business. Imagine the stomach it would take to say, "Well, I know this is morally suspect, but I'm doing it anyway, because I don't know how else to continue to support my family. God forgive me if forgiveness is in order!" Instead, the mind is taken hostage by the will, and a more palatable explanation is invented.

And of course there's nothing special about the real-estate business. We're constantly confronted with the opportunity to profit (financially or otherwise) from behavior that is morally suspect.

We rationalize to make life with ourselves possible in a morally challenging world.

Often the motivation for rationalization, though, is quite different. In recent decades, psychologists have argued convincingly that, more often than we think, we are guided not by reasons but by affect, emotion, and gut instinct. Interestingly, though, we tend to resist this explanation of our own beliefs and decisions. We prefer to think of ourselves as having conscious reasons for what we believe and what we do.

In one fascinating study, subjects were asked which of four garments they preferred. The garments were spread out from left to right. A noticeably disproportionate percentage — 40 percent — said that they preferred the rightmost garment. This confirmed what researchers had suspected: people tend to have an unconscious preference for things on their right. When asked why they chose the item they did, though, subjects quickly and confidently reported *reasons*. Some talked about the quality of the material, while others talked about the color — despite the fact that the four garments were made of the *same* material and were *identical* in color.

In "The Emotional Dog and Its Rational Tail,"[2] Jonathan Haidt has his subjects consider a story about a brother and sister who decide to engage in incest. The subjects are asked whether or not it is acceptable for two consenting adult siblings to have sex. Unsurprisingly, an overwhelming majority think not.

When asked why, though, things get a little dicey. Subjects first present *reasons* for thinking incest is inappropriate. When subjects are convinced that their reasons are faulty or inapplicable to the

2. Jonathan Haidt, "The Emotional Dog and Its Rational Tail: A Social Intuitionist Approach to Moral Judgment," *Psychological Review* 108 (2001): 814-34.

case under consideration, though, they don't abandon their conviction that incest is wrong. Instead, they frown and say, "I know it's wrong, I'm just having a hard time explaining why."[3]

Perhaps the reason people respond this way in Haidt's experiment is that there is no reason — no "why." More to the point, even if there *are* good reasons for thinking that incestuous sex is wrong, the average person's conviction on the matter is not a product of having worked through those reasons. She just knows. She can feel that it's wrong. She knows it "in her gut," as we often say.

If you're a Christian, you might think that you know it "because the Bible says so." But ask yourself: wouldn't you know it was wrong even if you didn't have the Bible to read? Does the Bible really function as the *source* of this belief for you? Or does the Bible simply confirm what you already know *in your gut* to be true?

Yet people are slow to present themselves as just knowing something like this "in their gut." Their first tack is to present themselves as knowing it on the basis of some reason or other. There is a kind of resistance to the idea that this thing is *just known,* and people are disappointed (hence the frown) when they can't articulate reasons. So subjects confabulate. They come up with reasons that (they hope) justify their conviction and present those reasons to themselves and others as the operative grounds for their judgment. But the reasons, as it turns out, are not responsible for the convictions. Rather, people just "feel" the wrongness of incestuous sexual relations. Arguments and reasons are an afterthought in an attempt to lend intellectual respectability to the gut reaction. And if the arguments that first come to mind don't turn the trick, they'll cast around for others that will.

3. Jonathan Haidt, *The Happiness Hypothesis* (New York: Basic Books, 2006), p. 21.

So we rationalize not only to make life with ourselves possible in a morally challenging world, but also out of a conviction that it *should* be reason that guides us and not our "gut." We've been convinced that unless our actions and beliefs arise out of considered reasons and arguments, they are somehow irrational or otherwise subpar.

Recently I saw a promotional flyer for a class pitched to young adults at a local church that had this heading: "Find Out WHY You Believe What You Believe." The flyer made it clear that the class would cover the various arguments for theism, for the reliability of Scripture, and for other matters of Christian conviction. But what a curious thing to find out from someone in a class! How do *they* know why *I* believe what I believe? I bet most of the people enrolled in the class had never heard of the arguments presented in the class prior to having attended. But then how could *these* be the reasons for *their belief*?

More likely than not, the answer to the question, "Why do you believe what you believe?" for most of those attending the class looks something like this: They believe what they do because their parents, teachers, and other authorities told them that it was true. And, moreover, it has always just *felt* right to them . . . in their gut, as it were. It just seems right, and the alternatives have always just seemed somehow wrong and implausible.

Of course, people who enroll in the class are not fooled by the flyer. They know that the cosmological argument, say, has not been among their reasons for believing that God exists. They're not tempted for a second to think of the class as simply unearthing what have been their reasons all along. They're coming to the class to *acquire* reasons for their conviction. But why? Well, surely for any number of reasons. But for some, the reason they've enrolled is because they think there's something irrational or otherwise inferior about believing that God exists without having good arguments. So they'll memorize the reasons and then present those reasons to themselves and others as though they're what lie back of the conviction they've had all along.

Now I don't mean to suggest that there's anything wrong with a class of this sort. I've been helped by classes like this, and I know others have, too. In fact, I teach classes like this from time to time. It's a faith-building exercise to learn of the evidence for the great truths of the gospel, and we're instructed to stand ready to make a defense for the hope that we have.

What I'm suggesting is that the class is not doing what it is sometimes thought of and advertised as doing. For the vast majority of Christians, it is not making clear why they believe what they believe. And it is not making rationally respectable Christians out of folks who were, before learning the arguments, somehow rationally or intellectually inferior with respect to their faith.

The thought that the class has these ends is fodder for the type of rationalization I'm talking about. If I think that belief is rational only to the extent that it is formed on the basis of good arguments, then I'll take a class like this and subsequently convince myself that my Christian beliefs are based on the arguments I've learned. But they're not. And the best evidence that they're not is that I'll be unlikely to abandon my beliefs when I encounter criticism of my new arguments for which I can't satisfy myself with a response. For most (though admittedly not all) belief persists even when the arguments are thought to have failed.

So we rationalize whenever we construct a rational justification for a belief, behavior, or decision arrived at by means other than the justification constructed. Sometimes we rationalize by switching to the perspective of another that better suits our purposes. Other times, we invent reasons and present them to ourselves and others as playing an explanatory role that they don't, in fact, play. Often, the idea that belief or conviction is irrational if it's not formed on the basis of considered reasons is what gives rise to rationalization. We grasp for any argument that makes sense of the conviction we already have and present it as explaining the fact that we believe what we do. And, in so doing, we deceive ourselves.

Ressentiment

Remember Aesop's Fox? Having spied some ripening grapes on a lofty branch, he tried with all his might to jump and take them. Once it dawned on him that he would not — could not — succeed, he sulked away, saying, "I'm sure they're sour anyway."

What about the reaction of the schoolboy whose fame owing to a cut finger suddenly waned when Tom Sawyer showed up with a new "talent," having just endured the trial of having his tooth pulled?[4]

> But all trials bring their compensations. As Tom wended to school after breakfast, he was the envy of every boy he met because the gap in his upper row of teeth enabled him to expectorate in a new and admirable way. He gathered quite a following of lads interested in the exhibition; and one that had cut his finger and

4. Mark Twain, *Tom Sawyer and Huckleberry Finn: The Adventures of Huckleberry Finn* (Hertfordshire: Wordsworth Editions, 1992), p. 33.

had been a centre of fascination and homage up to this time, now found himself suddenly without an adherent, and shorn of his glory. His heart was heavy, and he said with a disdain which he did not feel that it wasn't anything to spit like Tom Sawyer; but another boy said, "Sour grapes!" and he wandered away a dismantled hero.

We scorn what we cannot have because we cannot have it — even if, were it available to us, we would find it immensely attractive. Often the objects of our sour grapes are relatively insignificant — even trifling. We mock the man with the Rolex for paying so much for an instrument that keeps time no better than a Casio. We extol our secondhand junker for accomplishing everything that cars are supposed to accomplish ("it gets me wherever I need to go," we say) and wonder how anyone could bring themselves to make car payments that exceed our monthly rent.

Sometimes, though, the issues are much deeper. In *Notes from the Underground,* Dostoyevsky's narrator catches himself crying sour grapes over the naiveté enjoyed by the ordinary man.[5] The heightened consciousness of the underground man fates him to a recognition of his own passive inertia — his own powerlessness over life's course. So he wants to — tries to — accept that recognition as his settled preference. Better to be conscious of one's own personal insignificance than to be taken in by the illusion of freedom. But he can't quite break free of the desire for something more. Listen to his struggle:

5. Fyodor Dostoyevsky, *Notes from the Underground in Three Short Novels* (New York: Anchor Books, 1960), p. 211.

The long and the short of it is, gentlemen, that it is better to do nothing! Better conscious inertia! And so hurrah for underground! Though I have said that I envy the normal man to the last drop of my bile, yet I should not care to be in his place such as he is now (though I shall not cease envying him). No, no; anyway the underground life is more advantageous. There, at any rate, one can . . . Oh, but even now I am lying! I am lying because I know myself that it is not underground that is better, but something different, quite different, for which I am thirsting, but which I cannot find! Damn underground!

I will tell you another thing that would be better, and that is, if I myself believed in anything of what I have just written. I swear to you, gentlemen, there is not one thing, not one word of what I have written that I really believe. That is, I believe it, perhaps, but at the same time I feel and suspect that I am lying like a cobbler.

Crying sour grapes is one form of what Friedrich Nietzsche (and later Max Scheler) called "Ressentiment" — a re-ordering of the sentiments. We adjust our affections, sentiments, and value judgments in order to avoid severe disappointment or self-censure. When we cry sour grapes, we avoid the severe disappointment of not having what we want by convincing ourselves that we don't really want it after all. Often the ploy for discrediting the desired object is to place inordinate value on something else instead. We "take lemons and make lemonade." We fix our affections upon the paper-thin silver lining in hope of losing sight of the ominous dark cloud. Nietzsche famously attributes the Christian praise of humility and prizing of suffering to the ressentiment of the persecuted church. Since they could expect no better than humiliation and suffering, he said, the Christians re-ordered their sentiments in such a way as to praise humility and prize affliction.[6]

I've driven old cars for most of my adult life. Two of my favorites have been handed down to me by grandmothers who could no longer drive. The first was a gray 1980 Chevy Citation, complete with sport louvers on the back window. I sold that one for five hundred dollars when a cream-colored 1982 Oldsmobile Cutlass Ciera came my way from another aging grandmother. My neighbors drive nice cars. But I wouldn't have traded with them for the world. Just think of the advantages! I never worried about my cars being stolen, dinged, or scratched. In fact, I took great pleasure every time I let the cart bump ever so lightly against the side panel of my car as I approached to unload my groceries. I parked without fear in the tightest of spaces and never locked the doors. I could change lanes with hardly a glance, knowing that the driver next to me had more to lose. I never had to wash my cars — it wouldn't have made much of an improvement if I did. And I saved money on gas, not so much because the cars got good mileage, but because, when carpooling, nobody ever wanted me to drive. And then there's the all-important appearance of being untouched by the materialistic rat race that drives people to own nicer and nicer cars. I looked positively desert-fathers saintly driving around in my beaters. Yes, I loved those cars.

My world crashed in on me when my parents offered me a ridiculously good deal on their mint-condition 1999 Jeep Grand Cherokee with four-wheel drive, leather interior, and seats that adjust electronically. I was, at first, sad to say goodbye to my

6. Friedrich Nietzsche, *Beyond Good and Evil*, trans. Marion Faber (New York: Oxford University Press, 2008); see esp. chapter 3, "The Religious Disposition," and chapter 5, "Toward a Natural History of Morals."

Oldsmobile. Honestly, I was. But it would have been the height of financial irresponsibility to turn down the Jeep, so I condescended to my parents' generous offer.

Of course, after a year of driving the Jeep, I am now fully alive to the self-deluded re-ordering of values that made possible my preference for those old cars. So it goes in ressentiment. We adjust our preferences and values to accommodate whatever is realistic for us.

In the decades leading up to the turn of the twentieth century, ideas emerged in the centers of higher learning that seemed to many people as though they threatened the tenets of Christian orthodoxy. Darwin's theory of evolution seemed to call into question the Christian narrative concerning the nature and origin of man. At about the same time, "higher criticism" of the biblical text seemed to call into question the Christian narrative concerning the inspiration of Scripture. To some it seemed that more learning made the traditional Christian story less plausible. It began to look as though the flourishing of the intellect carried with it the rejection of traditional Christian narratives.

Well-intentioned Christian people found themselves with a perceived choice between full engagement with the growing body of knowledge in the main centers of higher learning and fidelity to their Christian commitments. Many of them chose the latter. And they cried sour grapes about the now seemingly unavailable life of the developed and educated mind. Like Aesop's Fox, they walked away from mainstream higher education muttering to themselves that the educated mind is a sour thing anyway.

So was born a pernicious anti-intellectualism in many corners of the Christian world that, in various forms and degrees, lives on to this day. In its more overt manifestations, it appears as an outright suspicion of higher education. It is nicely embodied in Flannery O'Connor's barber who "didn't have to read nothin'. All he had to do was think." In his tirade against education, he explains, "that was the trouble with people these days — they didn't think, they didn't use their horse sense. . . . Nossir! Big words don't do nobody no good. They don't take the place of thinkin'."[7]

Louis, a dear Christian man in my acquaintance, just loves to think. But, to his mind, the ideas that constitute the mainstream in centers of higher education — even Christian higher education — are incommensurate with Christian conviction. So for him higher education has become a danger. When he learns that someone has a Ph.D., even if it's from a Christian institution, he believes he has a reason for suspecting that what that person says is false. He's accepted a dichotomy that the vast majority of Christians down through the ages would have thought utterly absurd: that you must choose between a robust education and fidelity to the faith. Having chosen fidelity, he is sour on what would otherwise have been an immensely attractive course of life for him — a life of continual and robust intellectual training.

In its more subtle manifestations, anti-intellectualism discredits the life of the mind under the guise of super-valuing some-thing *else* — usually something legitimately valuable like faith, relationship, or "the heart," as if these could flourish without the development of the mind.

In Jane Austen's *Mansfield Park,* Edmond finds himself disillusioned with the former woman of his dreams.[8] Severe disappointment with the charming and aggressively extroverted Mary

---

7. Flannery O'Connor, "The Barber," in *The Complete Stories* (New York: The Noonday Press, 1993), p. 17.

8. Jane Austen, *Mansfield Park* (New York: E. P. Dutton & Co., 1906), p. 491.

Crawford causes him to wonder whether another sort of woman might do just as well, or even better. And then it dawns on him that Fanny Price, a woman quite Mary Crawford's opposite, for whom he functioned as a sort of big brother, might do very well indeed.

Having already developed an attachment to her in his big-brotherly role,

> what was there now to add, but that he should learn to prefer soft light eyes to sparkling dark ones. And being always with her, and always talking confidentially, and his feelings exactly in that favourable state which a recent disappointment gives, those soft light eyes could not be very long in obtaining the pre-eminence. Having once set out, and felt that he had done so on this road to happiness, there was nothing on the side of prudence to stop him or make his progress slow; no doubts of her deserving, no fears of opposition of taste, no need of drawing new hopes of happiness from dissimilarity of temper . . . timid, anxious, doubting as she was. . . .

It was his disappointment with Mary Crawford that positioned Edmond so favorably to give preeminence to the "soft light eyes" and "timid, anxious, doubting" disposition of Fanny Price. The qualities that once drew Edmond to Mary Crawford were not so much considered sour (say, recast as vices) as forgotten altogether. They simply faded from view in the wake of the re-ordering of affections in the direction of Fanny Price's temperament.

Postmodern culture generally — and postmodern Christian culture in particular — is profoundly disillusioned with the capacity of the mind's reasoning ability as a force for the good.

4370

The Enlightenment (against which postmodernism is a reaction) was a period in history characterized by an unbridled optimism concerning human reason. Caught up in the enthusiasm over the new philosophy spawned by the work of René Descartes and the explosive progress in the sciences, Enlightenment thinkers were tempted to conclude that if only the world would think and reason properly, we would find our way into a utopian kind of existence.

Nowhere is this more evident than in Baruch Spinoza's vision for philosophy and science done well. In his treatise *On the Improvement of the Understanding,* he explains that philosophy and science done well would enable him "to enjoy continuous, supreme, and unending happiness."[9] Not a bad goal.

But the increasing knowledge characteristic of the rise of the "new science" and Cartesian philosophy did not culminate in continuous, supreme, and unending happiness. Instead, as postmodernists never tire of reminding us, it gave us Hiroshima. Of course, it gave us much that is good too. But to the postmodern mind, the rise of science and the accumulation of knowledge is now recognizable as being subject to the whims of human management and mismanagement. Increased knowledge is no guarantee of a better world. To live in a postmodern culture is to be alive to the failure of reason and knowledge to live up to their Enlightenment expectations.

Like Edmond's disappointment with Mary Crawford, it is the postmodern disappointment with reason that positions it so favorably to give preeminence to matters of feeling and affection. In Christian circles, this emphasis on feeling is then associated

9. Benedictus de Spinoza, *Ethics: Preceded by On the Improvement of the Understanding* (New York: Simon and Schuster, 1970), p. 3.

— mistakenly — with the biblical emphasis on faith and the heart. It's not so much that reason is demonized, as it is in the more overt manifestation of anti-intellectualism discussed above, but that it is neglected altogether in favor of talk of feelings and affections. A sharp division is drawn between what is called "the mind" (usually pointing to the head) and what is called "the heart" (usually pointing to the chest), and nearly exclusive emphasis is given to "the heart."

But much that we describe as happening "up here" (pointing to our head), like "understanding things," "considering things," and "knowing things," is described in the biblical text as happening in the *heart*. The idea that the heart is primarily (or exclusively!) an instrument of feeling is simply not faithful to the biblical use of the term. So this particular manifestation of ressentiment, like so many others, calls for reinforcement from attention management. Those passages which describe the affective components of "the heart" are made the primary objects of focus in order to accommodate ressentiment in the direction of a feelings-centered Christianity.

So far, then, I have described two forms of ressentiment. In the first, a generally recognized good is made an object of outright scorn for its unavailability. In the second, a seemingly unavailable good is pushed to the edges of consciousness by super-valuing something else. We see both kinds of ressentiment in the various forms of Christian anti-intellectualism.

There is one final form that ressentiment can take. In this final form, it's not so much that there is an unavailable good creating a demand for the re-ordering of sentiments. It is rather that particular sentiments are deemed unacceptable, inappropriate, inconvenient, or otherwise undesirable. They are then recast as something other than what they are. They go undercover. They continue to operate, but they are renamed in such a way as to make them acceptable to the person who has them.

"I'm concerned about Steve," says Aaron at the weekly prayer meeting. "I think he's really gone off the deep end, and I'm afraid he's headed for trouble. I think we should pray for him." He spends the next half-hour explaining in some detail Steve's mistaken beliefs, his bad behavior, and the inevitable pain in store for Steve because of the course he's taken. Occasionally, a stray sarcastic comment bleeds through the otherwise sterile description of Steve's misfortune. But everything is presented as an articulation of his concern for Steve's well-being and an invitation to pray for him.

"How have you personally been affected by Steve's course?" asks Dan.

Aaron explains that there were some early interactions that were deeply hurtful. Steve had said some pretty nasty things, he explains. At first, he was angry. But he's forgiven Steve, and now he's mostly just concerned for Steve's well-being. Everyone buys his answer. After all, many of them have been hurt by similar interactions with Steve, and they can relate. They have forgiven him too. Finally someone suggests that they should actually get down to praying. So they do, and for the next seven minutes or so, a summary version of Steve's failings is presented to God as evidence that Steve is in need of rescue.

Mike Martin nicely describes the process involved in this third form of ressentiment:[10]

---

10. Mike Martin, *Self-Deception and Morality* (Lawrence: University Press of Kansas, 1986), p. 35.

It begins when a person experiences intense feelings of hatred in the form of envy, spite, or vindictiveness. Normal outward expression of the hatred is blocked because of fear and a felt lack of strength to display it before others. Gradually a process of repression occurs in which negative emotions and their specific objects are less readily available to consciousness. Focused hate is replaced by general negativism and malice that spill over into patterns of vicious criticism, cruelty, or betrayal. These indirect outlets do not remove the suppressed hate, however, which continues to smolder unattended to.

As it turns out, Aaron's still mad at Steve. He knows that he's supposed to forgive Steve, and he believes that if he's forgiven someone, he can't be mad at that person anymore. So he must choose between thinking of himself as not having really forgiven Steve or as not being mad at Steve anymore. He chooses the latter. But the anger still operates. It drives him to constant criticism, cynicism, and vindictiveness toward Steve.

So Aaron has re-cast his anger toward Steve as "concern." Concern is a convenient disguise for anger, since "concern" for someone is a perfectly legitimate sentiment, and it seems to justify many of the behaviors one would expect from someone who's just plain hurt and mad. Interestingly, his friends, who would recognize the ruse in almost any other situation (the occasional sarcasm is a dead giveaway), are slow to detect anger's covert operation, since they are caught up in the same ressentiment. They're angry with Steve, too. Were they to recognize it in Aaron, though, their own game would be up. So they reinforce one another's pretense that it is "concern" that motivates the discussion, and they congratulate themselves for having done Steve a service by bringing his sad case before the Lord.

When we're angry with others and we're not willing to think of ourselves as harboring anger toward them, we'll find some alternative characterization of our affective posture toward them. Sometimes we're "concerned" for them. Other times we're "sad." We're not angry with them; we just feel sorry for them. Or maybe we're frightened that someone else may be injured by their actions. "I'm not angry with him," we say. "I'm just worried that he's going to hurt someone else — something needs to be done to stop him."

The same is likely to occur in connection with any affective response deemed inappropriate or otherwise unattractive to the person who has it. Envy is another primary example. I can't stop thinking about Brian's brand-new wall-mounted flat-screen TV. It's not that I'm jealous. I'm just worried about Brian. Didn't he and Bethany already watch too much TV to begin with? This high-definition temptress is just going to lure them into more and more mindless entertainment of the sort that rots the soul. And what about poor Isaac, their ten-month-old little boy? He'll grow up in a living room that has a huge television (of all things!) as the focal point. What sort of impression is that likely to leave on his heart? Yep, somebody's got to talk to Brian. This is absolutely no good for him.

So ends our survey of the primary strategies for self-deception. Subtle strategies are required, because without them we're likely to catch ourselves in the act. But even these strategies are often insufficient to do the trick. Sometimes we're confronted so squarely with evidence against our favored belief that we're incapable of resisting. Fortunately, there's more that can be done. When I'm incapable of deceiving myself alone, I can solicit help from my friends and neighbors. In chapter five, we'll explore the social dynamics of self-deception. All too often we're willing participants and accomplices in one another's self-deceptive projects. It's much easier to deceive myself when I'm not working at it alone.

CHAPTER 5

Getting Help When
It's Not Working

T HE CONFUCIAN PHILOSOPHER MENGZI taught that every-one has within them a "seed" of morality. The key to virtue, he thought, was to identify the seed and to cultivate an environ-ment conducive to its growth. The seed reveals itself, according to Mengzi, by means of "giveaway actions." A giveaway action is an unreflective response that lays bare a conviction that runs contrary to the agent's articulated view. A person might say, for example, "I'm only interested in looking out for numero uno." But when she happens by a small child drowning in a mud swamp, she's likely to jump in, nice outfit and all, to rescue the child. It's a giveaway that the seed of selflessness is there despite protestations to the contrary. It needs only to be identified and cared for if one is to become truly virtuous.[1]

The concept of a "giveaway action" gives us a tempting strategy for rooting out self-deception. If we are truly self-deceived, we are, of course, likely to be blind to our own giveaway actions. But per-haps we can solicit the eyes and ears of our friends and associates to unearth the forces moving in our psyche to which we ourselves

---

1. For a nice discussion of this theme in Mengzi, see Philip J. Ivanhoe, *Confucian Moral Self-Cultivation* (Indianapolis: Hackett, 2000), pp. 18-20.

are so blind. The key to avoiding self-deception, we might think, is to invite those close enough to have an eye on our actions and stated beliefs to identify the giveaway actions as they arise.

We are, after all, very good at noticing giveaway actions for the vices of others. Who hasn't noticed in another, for example, radical insecurity masquerading as egotistical self-praise? A one-sided inquiry to protect cherished beliefs? Or anger with an associate masquerading as concern? Avoiding self-deception, one might think, is as easy as surrounding myself with people willing to tell me the truth about me as they see it.

Things aren't quite so easy, though. As it turns out, the people with whom we surround ourselves are often complicit in our self-deceptive strategies. In fact, there are heights of self-deception only reachable with the help of others. Some of my giveaway actions are so obvious, it seems, as to be unmistakable even to me without serious and persistent help from others who are equally committed to their concealment. In fact, it is when self-deception requires obscuring the extremely obvious that I'll need assistance from a willing group of others to succeed.

Many of our self-deceptive strategies would simply fall flat were it not for the willing cooperation of our group. So it is to this social dynamic of self-deception that we now turn. "Madness," said Nietzsche, "is rare in individuals — but in groups . . . it is the rule."[2]

To be sure, groups, when they're functioning well, can be among our best defenses against vicious self-deception. But when group thinking is replaced by what psychologists call "groupthink," the results can be disastrous. Irving Janis begins his treatment of

---

2. Friedrich Nietzsche, *Beyond Good and Evil*, trans. Marion Faber (New York: Oxford University Press, 2008), Aphorism 156, p. 70.

groupthink by describing the case of Pitcher, Oklahoma. Daniel Goleman nicely summarizes the case as follows:

> In 1950 a local mining engineer warned the people of this small mining town to flee. An accident had virtually undermined the town; it might cave in any minute. The next day at the Lion's Club meeting, the town leaders joked about the warning. When one arrived wearing a parachute, they laughed and laughed. The message "it can't happen here" implicit in their hilarity was sadly contradicted within a few days: some of these same men and their families were killed in the cave-in.[3]

In the chapters that follow, Goleman offers a very nice discussion of the psychological research on groupthink. A few of the most telling cases are these:[4]

The Bay of Pigs: Immediately upon the failure of the attempted overthrow of Castro at the Bay of Pigs, John F. Kennedy is reported to have asked, "How could I have been so stupid as to let them go ahead?" Studies of the incident strongly suggest that groupthink contributed significantly to the fiasco. In the strategy meetings leading up to the attack, it was Richard Bissel of the CIA (a known confidant and longtime friend of Kennedy's) who presented the invasion plan. When Kennedy was perceived as being in strong agreement with Bissel, the other advisors in the group played along. Intelligence easily attainable (or even already attained) by members of the advisory counsel strongly suggesting that the inva-

3. Daniel Goleman, *Vital Lies, Simple Truths: The Psychology of Self-Deception* (New York: Simon and Schuster, 1985), p. 180, in reference to Irving Janis, *Victims of Groupthink* (Boston: Houghton Mifflin, 1983).

4. See Goleman, *Vital Lies, Simple Truths,* pp. 159-235, for a more detailed description of these and other cases.

sion would fail simply never found a voice. The feeling of euphoria in the wake of having won the presidential office, a latent feeling of invulnerability, reluctance to contradict a strong and charismatic leadership team, and the luring appeal of comfortable consensus conspired to suppress information that would surely have given any reasonable military strategist pause.

The success of the invasion depended, for example, on the assumption that there would be massive uprisings in response to the military action by an underground resistance to Castro throughout Cuba. Without these uprisings, the invasion didn't stand a chance, as the invasion force was outnumbered more than 140 to 1 by Castro's army. But there was no good reason for assuming the likelihood of the uprising. In fact, a careful poll from the year before revealed that the vast majority of Cubans were behind Castro.

Corporate Groupthink: Studies show that high-power leaders who show a preference for working with ingratiating subordinates are likely to generate (often unwittingly) contexts in which there is an illusion of unanimity. These leaders are rarely explicit in their discouragement of critique and dissent. They often present themselves as though they're seeking the voice and counsel of the group. Nevertheless, employees of such leaders understand that their success in the workplace depends not so much on how well they work together with other members of the group, but on the degree to which they fall in line with the leader. As a result, they're reluctant to voice critical feedback or dissenting opinions in meetings. Since others are similarly reluctant, there is the appearance of group unanimity in the direction of the leader's proposed course. While there are many with dissenting opinions, it looks to each as though everyone else is on board with the leader.

This perceived unanimity, then, causes individuals to doubt whatever critical thought they might have been having: "If everyone else is in agreement with this, maybe I'm just not seeing it clearly." As a result, not only is the thought not expressed at the meeting, it is discounted as invalid by the very person who has it. In the most extreme cases, the leader may then exploit the illusory unanimity. He may document it and give it overt articulation to reinforce the good judgment reflected in compliance: "We've all had a chance to look at this, and it sounds like we're all in agreement to move forward." To the extent that all of this occurs, the group ceases to function as a group and functions instead to reinforce and solidify whatever blind spots were the leader's to begin with.

The Game of Happy Family: Most families have tacit rules that govern what can and cannot be said, acknowledged, attended to, and done. These rules constitute the game of Happy Family. It is essential to the game of Happy Family, though, that the rules of Happy Family remain tacit. To acknowledge them would indirectly call attention to that which the rules are intended to keep hidden. R. D. Laing summarizes the rules of the Happy Family game as follows:[5]

Rule A: Don't.

Rule A.1:   Rule A doesn't exist.

Rule A.2:   Do not discuss the existence or nonexistence of Rules A, A.1, or A.2.

Anyone who has endured life with an alcoholic or an abusive parent or spouse will recognize immediately the operation of these rules. Simple survival requires that certain realities are obscured

5. R. D. Laing, *The Politics of the Family* (Toronto: CBC Publications, 1969), p. 41.

from vision. But the realities are so forcefully present in experience that they can be ignored only with the cooperation of the group. We must all collude to ignore this reality and then agree to take no notice of the collusion. Once broken free of the blinding forces of the Happy Family game, victims of abuse are often astounded at what they experienced but disregarded.

I live in Orange County, California. Have for most of my life. By any reasonable standard, Orange County is one of the very richest regions in the history of human existence — not just one of the richest in the world, but one of the richest in the *history* of the world. I'm surrounded by people with wealth beyond the wildest imagination of most people who've ever lived. But these same people struggle with discontent over the material possessions they don't yet posses.

I'm one of those people. For the past two weeks, I've checked Craigslist every single day — often multiple times during the day — for a table saw. I don't have a project going just now that requires a table saw. But I'm just itching to have one and would be oh-so-much-happier if I had one in my garage.

Materialism is epidemic in my culture. By any reasonable standard, virtually all of the people in my immediate acquaintance are hoarding and storing up treasure on earth. We can't go for any appreciable period of time without a new purchase of some significance.

The Bible is clear, it seems to me, that this kind of materialism is a crippling barrier to the way of Jesus. Jesus taught that your heart will follow your treasure . . . automatically, as it were. The teaching suggests, at the very least, that it is *extremely* difficult to have treasure without growing attached to it in your heart in a way that precludes full participation in the way of Jesus. So I live in a context in which the dangers associated with having one's heart carried away by wealth loom larger than they have in virtually every other society in the history of the world.

But I've attended churches in Orange County nearly my whole life, and I can count with just my fingers the sermons I can remember directly calling attention to this epidemic in our midst. We have, it seems to me, decided together to be blind to the exorbitance of the average Orange County lifestyle. We'll challenge one another to tithe, of course, and to give generously to good causes. The assumption in our midst is that if I am making it a practice to give generously, I am free from the most crippling effects of materialism — even if my lifestyle belies a sort of addiction to expensive entertainment, conspicuous consumption, and regularly buying new and nice things for myself.

If you want to ruffle feathers in an Orange County church, raise the question of whether buying a new BMW can be justified in our world economy. You don't even have to present an answer; simply raising the question violates the game of Happy Family we're playing together with respect to nice cars — not to mention entertainment, fine foods, new appliances, and so much more.

Rule A: Don't question the moral legitimacy of buying a
             new BMW.
Rule A.1:   Rule A doesn't exist.
Rule A.2:   Do not discuss the existence or nonexistence of
             Rules A, A.1, or A.2.

Interestingly, it's those who spend time away from the "family" that find themselves painfully aware of the game we're playing. Folks who come home from short-term missions trips to Third

World countries find themselves wanting to violate Rule A. They often struggle with the moral legitimacy of Orange County life-styles — at least for a time. But, if they're typical, they can be brought back into the family. Procrastination will prevent them from really *doing* anything with these moral convictions. And the perceived unanimity of the group as to the insignificance of the question (whether it's okay to buy a new BMW) will cause it to fade to the edges of consciousness, where it will be less disruptive.

Notice, though, the absolutely essential place of my group if I'm going to continue to think that the question is insignificant — that there's no pressing need to ask it. If you plop me down in just about any other social context in the history of the world, the relative expense required to purchase a new BMW would raise questions so obvious as to be impossible to ignore. The opportunity costs of owning a new BMW (as opposed to a Honda Accord, for example) measured in terms of shareable basic necessities are staggering. It's only in a world of other BMW owners who've agreed not to ask the question that I could possibly ignore it. And of course the same may be true, though to a lesser extent, of the opportunity costs of owning a new Honda Accord as opposed to an economy car or a used car.

This is why the lifestyle in the next stratum up from wherever you're situated will look to you as though it teeters on the edge of exorbitance and gross materialism — but it won't look so to those situated *there*. For them, it will be the strata above them that satis-fies that description. We surround ourselves with those willing to ignore the questions with respect to our particular standard of living. In so doing, we make possible a blindness not otherwise possible to the grip of materialism. The last thing a rich man wants to do is to accuse his rich neighbor of being too rich.

The same is true, arguably, with respect to vanity and the obsession with physical appearance. The amount of time, money, energy, and thought devoted to getting all the bumps in proper proportion and all the colors just right seems absurd to anyone not sufficiently immersed in our culture of fixation on body image. But when is the last time you heard a sermon asking whether Christians, as a matter of course, should be pursuing cosmetic surgery, Botox, or abnormally large biceps? We've tacitly agreed to leave these issues unaddressed, and only the uninitiated will think to ask them. Meanwhile, body obsession squelches the well-intentioned efforts of millions to follow the way of Jesus fully.

There is a Christian radio station in my area that prides itself in being "family friendly." They advertise themselves this way, presumably, because they don't allow any sexually explicit material across their airwaves. So we're supposed to be able to listen without having to censure for the sake of preserving our kids' naiveté. But when I listen to "family friendly" radio stations with my six-year-old son in the car, I find myself having to answer questions like these: Why would I want to look younger than I am, Daddy? What's wrong with having wrinkles under your eyes, Daddy? What does it mean to look good in your bikini, Daddy? Why would I take a vitamin in order to eat less? Why wouldn't I just eat less?

It's not just that I hear *as much* of this on Christian radio as I do on other radio stations. I hear *more* of it. These advertisers are not in the charity business; they know what they're doing. So it seems Christians in my area have presented themselves to the marketplace as especially easy targets for this sort of thing.

But we never talk about it in church. We've agreed not to talk about it. And we've agreed not to call attention to the fact that we don't talk about it. But all the while, folks are routinely crippled in their pursuit of Jesus by body mania of such an extreme variety as to be evident to anyone outside the "family."

Groupthink shows up, too, in the context of personal relationships. We've already seen how a common ressentiment in a group can lead to collective blindness. Aaron's entire prayer group manifests a kind of collective blindness to the anger they all harbor toward Steve. They had all agreed that they had forgiven Steve — isn't that what Christians do, after all? — and that having forgiven him, they were no longer angry with them. All the while, though, collective anger and resentment continued to fuel a negative, cynical spirit toward Steve.

Recently, I attended a Sunday school class in a Pentecostal church dealing with the question of healing. The teacher was masterfully introducing the class to the deep truth that God is still working in the world — that he still wants to do in the world what he started to do in the ministry of Jesus and the apostles. He spoke out of decades of powerful experience, and folks in the class were coming alive to the exciting possibility that God would work powerfully in our midst, right here, today. As a part of the discussion, the teacher was inviting us to expect and pray for acts of supernatural healing in our midst. On the white board in the front of the class was displayed a text from James 5:

> Are any among you suffering? They should pray. Are any cheerful? They should sing songs of praise. Are any among you sick? They should call for the elders of the church and have them pray over them, anointing them with oil in the name of the Lord. The prayer of faith will save the sick, and the Lord will raise them up; and anyone who has committed sins will be forgiven. Therefore confess your sins to one another, and pray for one another, so

that you may be healed. The prayer of the righteous is powerful and effective.

The teacher encouraged faith in the real possibility of healing by offering a couple of stories from his experience. They were powerful stories, and I found myself stimulated to greater effort in praying for the sick. I don't think I was alone. The teacher was also honest, though, about times when he'd prayed for healing and God had said No. He suggested — rightly, I think — that we should pray in faith that God can do anything and trust that God has our ultimate best interest in mind. But there is no promise that if we somehow get the prayer formula just right, the healing will come.

Then a hand went up. Someone in the audience asked a question about the James passage on the board. "That passage in James sure *looks* like a promise. Why are we told that the prayer offered in faith will restore the one who is sick if that's not true?" Not a bad question. Why doesn't the passage say, "and the prayer offered in faith will save the one who is sick, and the Lord will raise him up if he deems it in everyone's best interest"? Wouldn't that have caused a lot less confusion? As it stands, it looks like we have to choose between (i) thinking of ourselves as praying wrongly (without faith) whenever healing doesn't occur, (ii) thinking of James as having stated things misleadingly, or (iii) sidestepping and collectively ignoring the fact that this looks very much like an unfulfilled promise in Scripture.

The teacher reiterated several aspects of his experience with prayer — sometimes its desired effect came, and sometimes it didn't. He suggested that we're often not privy to God's plan. And he encouraged us to do our part in prayer knowing that God is good and is working all things to a beautiful and redeeming end. I sat behind the man who asked the question, so I couldn't read his facial expression. Immediately, though, audible agreement rippled through the audience, indicating a general satisfaction with the response. Several more hands went up, and each subsequent contribution to the discussion confirmed God's healing power by means of a personal story of God's healing. We were quickly taken back to our project — cultivating the expectation that God will move powerfully in our midst.

Now I don't mean to criticize the teacher's answer. I believe everything the teacher said, and I'm not sure I could have done much better on the spot. What is remarkable in this context is the response of the class. After all, the question as to what to do with this passage in James was never addressed. I don't think the teacher *intentionally* avoided the question, but he avoided it nevertheless. Now, people generally know when a question they've asked gets sidestepped. When you ask the salesman how much the refrigerator costs, and he goes on for ten minutes about its bells and whistles and about how you'd pay much more for it down the street, you feel immediately dissatisfied. "Yeah . . . but how much does it *cost*?" If he sidesteps again, chances are you'll go down the street. Remarkably, though, Christians will often go their entire lives having questions like the one asked in this Sunday school class sidestepped — without so much as realizing that it's happening.

How can we have our questions so thoroughly sidestepped without noticing? Are our pastors and teachers such skilled politicians? I don't think so. They are able to sidestep our questions only with our collective cooperation. We're not quite willing to ignore the questions altogether. Somehow we feel that they ought to be asked. But when the question concerns a cherished belief, we're ready to accept an otherwise unsatisfying response.

Perhaps, if I'm the one who asked the question, I'll have a moment of felt dissatisfaction. "Yeah, but what should we do with this passage in James?" But the audible nods of agreement and satisfaction from the group will likely bring me back into line. "Everyone else seems satisfied. Perhaps I'm just not seeing it right. Or maybe I'm being needlessly skeptical."

In his work on groupthink, Irving Janis has identified eight symptoms of the phenomenon, some of which have already been apparent in our discussion. Together they constitute a sort of watch list for groupthink.[6]

1. Illusion of invulnerability: excessive optimism that encourages taking extreme risks.

2. Collective rationalization: members discount warnings and do not reconsider their assumptions.

3. Belief in inherent morality: members believe in the rightness of their cause and therefore ignore the ethical or moral consequences of their decisions.

4. Stereotyped views of out-groups: negative views of the "enemy" make effective responses to conflict seem unnecessary.

5. Direct pressure on dissenters: members are under pressure not to express arguments against any of the group's views.

6. Self-censorship: doubts and deviations from the perceived group consensus are not expressed.

---

6. Irving Janis, *Victims of Groupthink* (Boston: Houghton Mifflin, 1972; rev. ed., 1983). See Goleman, *Vital Lies, Simple Truths*, pp. 186-89, for a concise summary of these themes.

7. Illusion of unanimity: the majority view and judgments are assumed to be unanimous.

8. Self-appointed "mindguards": members protect the group and the leader from information that is problematic or contradictory to the group's cohesiveness, view, and/or decisions.

The third symptom bears special mention in our discussion. Victims of groupthink tend to exhibit decreased moral sensitivity to actions and decisions which might otherwise present themselves as clearly out of bounds. This will be especially true when the group is unified by a commitment to a big and seemingly righteous cause. The bigger and more urgent the cause, the more likely we are to be dead to the moral value of anything — or anyone! — perceived as standing in its way. This seems to be especially true if the cause is "religious." Blaise Pascal said it well: "We never do evil so fully and cheerfully as when we do it out of conscience."[7]

I've got a friend who brings levity during the workday to countless associates by passing along Internet humor in the form of a "Joke-of-the-Day" (JOTD). Sometimes it's a picture. Sometimes it's a video or a one-liner. Often it's funny. Sometimes it makes me cringe. On occasion, it makes me wish I didn't have email.

In recent months, several of these JOTDs have taken aim at the moral integrity, intelligence, and overall basic humanity of the Iraqi people. One includes graphic footage of a handful of Iraqi insurgents trying to figure out how to use a handheld missile launcher. After some fumbling around, it explodes and leaves no discernible trace of the Iraqis. In another, a U.S. military officer

7. Blaise Pascal, *Pensees*, trans. A. J. Krailsheimer (New York: Penguin Books, 1966), no. 813, p. 272.

is seen questioning an Iraqi citizen at a checkpoint as to the location of his "friends" the Iraqi insurgents. The young man in the car speaks no English, is clearly nervous, and simply wants to get through the checkpoint. The officer holds him there and lectures him (in English) about the fact that none of his "friends" have been out to play. He asks him to extend an invitation to his "friends" to come out and play very soon — before his shift at the checkpoint is up. There is tangible contempt — not only for the insurgency, but for this Iraqi citizen — in the officer's voice and posture.

A mock advertisement for Volkswagen has this title: "Iraqi intelligence meets German Engineering." In it, an Iraqi man parks his new VW next to a curbside restaurant in a busy suburban area. Sitting in the car with a bomb strapped to his chest, he pushes the detonator. We hear a muffled "poof" and see an explosion inside the car that leaves everyone and everything outside the car untouched. The most recent offering has a U.S. military officer in the foreground leading the Iraqi guard in an exercise routine beginning with jumping jacks. The email has this subject line: "Why the U.S. will never be able to leave Iraq." The scene resembles almost exactly what I saw when I watched my five-year-old son's soccer coach lead his team in the same exercise.

Now I'm not prepared to give an argument for or against our war efforts in Iraq. I doubt I know enough to have a strong opinion about the wisest course of action in that situation. I do know, though, that it would be easier to live with the consequences of our nation's chosen course of action were we to think of Iraqis as somehow below the threshold of normal humanity. It's easier to buy the idea that they're in desperate need of our continued supervision, for example, if we think of them as operating with the intelligence and coordination of an average American five-year-old.

It's easier to live with the atrocities of war if we collectively decide to think of our enemies as stupid and immoral.

Of course, if asked whether or not most Iraqi citizens are stupid and immoral, most people will have enough sense to say No. But subtle group mechanisms, like those at work in the JOTDs, allow those assumptions to function without being explicitly endorsed. The stereotyping on display in these emails would be recognized by most in today's race-sensitive environment as clearly out of bounds were it not for its service to a big, expensive, and "righteous" cause.

A recently released documentary has as its purpose to expose an uncritical bias in the mainstream scientific community against the hypothesis that the universe owes its existence to an intelligent designer. Apparently, scientists exploring this hypothesis in their theoretical research have on several occasions been blackballed by their guild. The documentary represents an attempt to awaken the general public to this impediment to scientific inquiry.

Much of the movie is given over to the project of associating opponents of intelligent design with the oppressive practices of Nazi Germany and the Soviet Bloc. The video consistently goes back and forth between interview footage and images of Nazi oppression or the Berlin Wall. In addition to the images, there is an extended exploration of the connection between Darwinism and the atrocities of Nazi Germany. Of course, you're as unlikely to find an intelligent Darwinist scientist endorsing Nazism as you are to find an intelligent Christian endorsing the atrocities of the Crusades or the Ku Klux Klan. Nevertheless, the movie seeks repeatedly to create and reinforce the Darwinism/Nazism connection. The result, if one takes the film to heart, is an impression of Darwinist scientists according to which they're oblivious to obvious evidence and teetering on the edge of moral collapse of the sort we encountered in the Second World War.

As you might expect, enemies of intelligent design are equally busy questioning the intelligence and moral integrity of their opposition. Books and movies that belittle religious perspectives as uniformly deluded and even dangerous are suddenly popular. From a certain distance, the whole thing looks like just so much grade-school-playground bad blood.

Now, as a Christian, I do believe that the universe owes its existence to an intelligent designer. It wouldn't be at all surprising, moreover, to learn of the existence of scientific evidence for the existence of this creator. And I'm against the vilification and professional persecution of scientists who take this possibility seriously. But shouldn't we stand equally opposed to vilification and lack of charity in the other direction? Arguably, devotion to a cause, even a very good cause, has the potential to blind us to what would otherwise be obvious facts — that the enemies of the intelligent-design movement (some of them, anyway) are incredibly bright and morally decent scholars who disagree with us. Were it not for our cause, we might even enjoy their company and take ourselves to have a great deal to learn from them. In an unguarded moment, we might even seek moral advice from them on a matter of common interest. But that sort of thinking doesn't rally the troops nearly so effectively as do subtle hints to the effect that our enemies are blind, stupid (though technically gifted, perhaps, in the way that autistic people are sometimes good at math), or morally suspect. And once we've got them in that camp, it will be easier to live with ourselves if our cause requires that we mock and ridicule them.

But of course it's not just in the context of Christian treatment of non-Christian opposition that we're likely to find vilification and mistreatment in the service of a cause. Sadly, Christians do this to each other. Consider any significant matter of disagreement between conservative and liberal Christians — homosexuality, war, women in ministry, the death penalty, you name it. In my experience, Christians on the conservative side of this issue are quick to portray their Christian opposition as, for example, careless in their biblical scholarship, blind to certain "obvious" natural-law observations, and questionable with respect to motives — "They're just trying to justify the pursuit of their own lusts." Of course, Christians on the liberal side of the issue are making similar accusations: their opponents are backward, insensitive, mean-spirited, bigoted. The result is reciprocal maltreatment back and forth among people who might well enjoy one another's company were it not for their allegiance to a cause. Since they're basically morally decent people all around, they'd never be caught treating others this way — except for the fact that they're devoted to a cause that seems to require it.

Back of much of this vilification and lack of charity is an implicit — and confused — argument about what should be concluded when sincere, intelligent, and equally informed people disagree about something. Many of us are tempted to think, mistakenly, that if sincere, intelligent, and equally informed people disagree about something, there must be no objective truth to the matter, or at least that the truth can't be known. But people *do* disagree with us. And there *is* an objective truth on the matter — and we're sure we know it. So the people who disagree with us must be either insincere, stupid, or ill-informed. Why else would they disagree?

We tend not to have a category for disagreement between equally sincere, intelligent, and well-informed people where there is a genuine and discoverable truth of the matter. And without such a category, we're faced with a choice between (i) giving up on the idea that we know the truth on the issue in question or (ii) thinking of our opponent as insincere, stupid, or ill-informed. If our cause is one that we cherish, the second option will be the more attractive. And once we've got our opponent characterized as insincere, stupid, or ill-informed, then mistreatment, mockery, and exclusion from serious discussion — all for the sake of the cause, of course — will come more easily.

I've never been on staff at a church. But everyone I know who has been seems to have a story to tell about the mistreatment of a Christian brother or sister for the sake of the good of the church. Nothing makes the mistreatment of another easier than a passionate commitment to an ideal that presents itself as more important than the people who stand in the way of its realization. What would present itself as obvious and egregious disrespect and mistreatment if considered alone is granted moral legitimacy by the group consciousness in devotion to a cause.

The past three chapters represent an attempt to canvass and illustrate the various forms that self-deception takes in the context of Christian culture. Very often, we can achieve the self-deception we require on our own. We manage our attention. We rationalize. We switch perspectives. We adjust our sentiments. We procrastinate. We combine methods to form strategies of staggering complexity. Sometimes, though, we need help. It is only in the context of groupthink and collective group commitments that certain acts of self-deception can be carried off.

My hope is to have said enough about each of the various forms of self-deception to make possible a consideration of the likelihood that self-deception is alive in your experience. I've done my job if you're beginning to think "I wonder if I've been altogether fair in my evaluation of the evidence for _____ or if I've been deceiving myself" or "I wonder if we've allowed ourselves to vilify or think and act uncharitably toward _____ in the service of our collective devotion to _____."

To state the obvious, the picture has not been pretty. This has been the bad-news part of the book. You might think it's starting to look as if we're all caught up in self-deception and there's very little we can do about it. Why, you might wonder, have we been created in such a way as to allow for this kind of pervasive breakdown in rationality?

Well, chapter six is the good news. On the one hand, there is the good news that our capacity for self-deception is God-given. He could have created us, after all, in such a way that our beliefs always correspond to the evidence. But he didn't. Presumably he had his reasons. What might they have been?

Reflection on the surprising fact that self-deception serves legitimate ends frees us up to recognize it in ourselves without crippling self-censure. And having eyes to see it is the first step in the direction of eliminating it in those areas of our lives where it doesn't belong.

CHAPTER 6

How-Not-To, Part 1: Giving Self-Deception a Demotion

S O FAR, IT'S A PRETTY bleak picture. More often than we'd like to think, we're caught up in an assortment of self-deceptive strategies. For a variety of reasons, we avoid the use of rational standards in the formation of our beliefs. We manage our attention in order *not* to see things. In our avoidance of the truth, we procrastinate, adjust our sentiments, rationalize, and switch perspectives. And when none of that works, we solicit the help of our fellow self-deceivers.

But then where can I turn for the truth? Not to myself. I am, after all, the culprit in this disaster. Not to my friends and family. They can, in many instances, be counted on to be complicit in the lie. To God? But how do I know I'm not just hearing what I want to hear from him as well?

So is it hopeless? What can be done about self-deception? The goal of this chapter is to present a strategy for making progress in moving away from self-deception.

To move away from self-deception, though, I'll need to have a balanced view of its role in human existence. As with most things, the first step in the movement away from self-deception is recognition. I'll need to learn to recognize my own self-deceptive strategies if I'm going to do battle with them. I'll need to come to grips with the possibility that I am significantly self-deceived. I'll need courage to admit that possibility and to conduct an honest search for the conditions in my own lived experience that make self-deception likely.

As was suggested in chapter one, though, I'll be less likely to come to grips with my own self-deceptive strategies if I've made *authenticity* chief among the virtues.

To return to our earlier example, someone who thinks racism isn't such a big deal won't have much trouble recognizing his own racist tendencies. Those of us who think that racism is a very big deal will likely have more trouble doing so. Similarly, if we didn't think all that much of authenticity and truth, we'd likely have less trouble identifying the inauthentic in ourselves. It would be less threatening to realize that we often have desires that trump our desire to know the truth and to be truthful with ourselves and others. But for those of us who think that authenticity and truth are very important, recognizing the inauthentic and deception in ourselves may be more difficult. For those who've elevated authenticity and truth above all else, recognizing self-deception may be nearly impossible.

Ironically, then, to increase the chances that we'll be able to recognize our own self-deceptive strategies, we may need to give self-deception a demotion in the order of vices. To do that, we must first say something briefly about the value of truth. Having put truth in its place, we'll want to say something about the positive value of the mechanisms that make self-deception possible — and even of self-deception itself. Once we've got a balanced view of self-deception, we'll be better positioned to see it in ourselves and do battle with it.

Putting Truth in Its Place

Just after the debacle with the golden calf and just before he receives the stone tablets, Moses has a fascinating and terrifying conversation with God. Caught up in gratitude for God's mercy, Moses makes the following request: "Show me your glory!" (Exodus 33:18). He wanted an unfiltered, direct acquaintance with God's goodness. He wanted the pure, naked, unqualified, unmediated truth. What does God's goodness look like when it's not veiled by clouds, fire, or anything else? That seems like a reasonable — even holy — thing to want.

The problem? It would have killed him. God knew it would have killed him and valued his survival above granting his request to see things as they are.

Knowing the truth is, in general, extremely important. But knowing the truth is not *all*-important. On occasion, we find that something else is more important. Terminal cancer wards are full of patients who believe things we all know to be radically improbable. They believe that they will be one of the very, very few who fight back and win — or that they'll be the recipient of a miracle healing in response to the prayers of friends and family. It's not just that they believe that they *could* get better — that God *could* perform a miracle on their behalf. In this they're surely correct. No. They believe they *will* get better — that God *will* perform a miracle on their behalf. Nearly all of them are wrong. And anyone familiar with the statistics is well situated to see that they are. But — and this is the salient part for our discussion — nobody corrects them. In fact, they are encouraged to persist in these highly improbable beliefs.

Ordinarily, if you have friends who believe something of great significance that is almost certainly false, you'll feel some pressure — rightly — to assist them in moving toward the truth. But not always. Sometimes there are more important things at stake. Truth is important, but it's not *all*-important. Sometimes failing to know what could be known contributes to human flourishing. Sometimes a decision *not* to know is the course of greatest wisdom. Wise parents, for example, do not know everything it is in their power to know about their kids. They create space for healthy parent/child relationships by leaving some things unknown — or at least at the child's discretion to reveal.

Interestingly, "curiosity" appears on the list of *vices* in classical Greek culture. To be curious — in the classical Greek context — is to pursue knowledge that isn't any good for you, knowledge better not had. Unlike the Greeks, we often forget that some things are better left unknown.

But didn't Jesus teach that the truth will set us free? Well . . . no, he didn't. Consider the text from which that teaching is usually extracted, John 8:31-32: "Then Jesus said to the Jews who had believed in him, 'If you continue in my word, you are truly my disciples; and you will know the truth, and the truth will make you free.'"

There's a big difference between telling you that I'll give you twenty dollars if you wash my car and telling you that I'll give you twenty dollars. The first bit of news is *conditional*. You get the twenty dollars but *only if* you wash my car.

Notice that the teaching in John 8 is also *conditional*. *If you continue in my word*, you will be my disciples, and you will know the truth, and the truth will set you free. Jesus promises that the truth will be freeing for the one who is continuing in his word. All bets are off for those who are not continuing in his word.

Presumably, Jesus knew that the truth can be life-destroying. It is only in the context of discipleship to Jesus that we can become persons increasingly capable of handling the truth. Someday we will see God face to face. No doubt, that will be an immensely freeing experience. But, like Moses, we're in no condition for that yet. Until that day, God has graciously arranged for us to be kept in the dark with respect to truths that would harm or destroy us.

William Clifford famously suggested that "it is wrong always, everywhere, and for anyone, to believe anything upon insufficient evidence."[1] On one way of reading this, it just means that if you don't believe according to the evidence, you're failing to live up to rational standards. On a stronger and more straightforward reading, it means not only that believing without sufficient evidence is contrary to rational standards, but also that it shouldn't be done — ever. But this stronger claim is surely wrong. There's nothing at all wrong with encouraging the cancer patient's belief that she'll be healed. In fact, there's some reason to think that if she believes she'll be healed, it'll be less radically improbable that she *will* be.

God created us in such a way that we are not slaves to rational standards for considering evidence. We are, within limits, free to believe things even when we know them to be highly improbable. He could have done otherwise. He could have created us in such a way that we always believe what our evidence supports. Presumably, then, while it was important to God that we be capable of believing what is true, it was not *all*-important to him that we *always* believe what is true.

In what follows, we'll consider some concrete suggestions as to why it is that God might have given us this capacity. What could

1. William Clifford, "The Ethics of Belief," in Louis Pojman, ed., *The Quest for Truth* (New York: Oxford University Press, 2002), p. 109.

possibly be more important than believing the truth? The story of Moses and our own reactions to cancer-ward patients give us at least the beginnings of an answer. It seems that, at least in some circumstances, we're willing to compromise knowing the truth for the sake of increasing our chances of sheer survival.

Beyond mere survival, there are important life projects that seem to require belief in the highly improbable. Even though he's failed countless times in the past, the drug addict manages to work up the belief that *this time* he'll quit. He's probably wrong. Nevertheless, the belief in question makes success less improbable. The belief is an important ingredient in the recipe for the *possibility* of success. And what about the addict's friend? Ought the friend to believe that he'll quit this time? Should he really believe? Or should he just feign belief in order to facilitate the attempt? Love hopes all things and believes all things. Love is optimistic. It is sometimes optimistic in the face of evidence that warrants pessimism. Perhaps loyalty and love sometimes require something less than perfectly rational standards for the beliefs we take on about those we love. The friend decides to believe that *this time* the addict will quit. The wife decides to believe that *this time* her husband will be faithful. The father decides to believe that *this time* his teen-aged son will handle freedom responsibly.

Misfiring Mechanisms

Before we discuss further the value of outright self-deception, though, consider a few of the mechanisms or capacities that give rise to acts of self-deception. The most interesting varieties of self-deception would be simply impossible were it not for our capacities for perspective switching, attention management, and procrastination. As a first step in achieving a balanced view of self-deception, consider the good things made possible by these amazing capacities.

Recently, Laurel and I rented the movie *Juno*. In it a pregnant and single teen-aged girl decides to carry her baby to term and give it up for adoption. Viewing the movie gave me a glimpse of the world from the perspective of a person in those circumstances. I'm not so naïve as to think that I now understand exactly what it must be like to be a pregnant teen-aged girl giving up her baby for adoption. But I did get closer to understanding. And insofar as I did, I positioned myself to be more sympathetic and loving to someone in those shoes.

Seeing the world from the perspective of another makes possible a kind of empathy that would be otherwise impossible. If I simply can't achieve any grasp at all of the world as it appears from your perspective, it will be hard for me to sympathize with you, love you, or interact with you as anything other than an alien. Often the first step toward forgiveness is to see the world from the perspective of the person wronging you — even if that perspective significantly distorts the truth. If I can see the world from your point of view, however distorted it may be, I may see that your behavior toward me is motivated by deep fear or hurt that has nothing to do with me at all. If I were incapable of adopting any perspective but the true one, I would be incapable of seeing me from your (distorted) point of view. And it is precisely the ability to see myself from your point of view that creates space in my heart to forgive you for your behavior towards me.

Much in the appreciation of great fiction presupposes the ability to adopt a perspective other than one's own. Moreover, it presupposes the ability to enter into a perspective without regard for whether the circumstances described are true. Movies like *Forrest Gump* or *The Green Mile* touch us deeply. We feel the deep movements of loyalty, friendship, justice, love, regret, and familial connection. But we feel all of these things by adopting the perspective of a character so far from the realm of plausibility and truth as to render silly any question of whether the story is true. Of course the same is true of books such as the *Chronicles of Narnia, Lord of the Rings*, and countless others. If I were incapable of adopting any perspective but my own, there would be nothing at all for me in these great works of fiction. The same would be true if I were incapable of entering into a perspective without regard for its literal truth.

Perspective switching, then, is an amazing God-given ability that allows me to empathize with people whose experiences hardly resemble my own. It smoothes the path to sympathy, pity, and forgiveness. And it is a prerequisite for the appreciation of great fiction. Though it can be requisitioned by the self-deceiver for ends unbecoming of its design, the capacity for perspective switching is one to be celebrated. Our lives are infinitely richer because of this ability to step out of our own shoes, temporarily disregard the question of truth, and see things from another point of view.

The same is true of attention management. The ability to restrict attention to a limited number of things at any given time is crucial for survival and basic proper function. At any given moment, I am assailed by countless sights and sounds. If I had no ability to focus my attention selectively, I would be incapable of carrying out even the most basic tasks of ordinary life. In fact, some learning disabilities are correlated with an inability to filter or block out sensory stimuli in order to focus on the task at hand.

Except in the most extreme cases, though, even folks with these learning disabilities retain the ability to focus attention selectively. If they didn't, they wouldn't be capable of simple tasks like driving a car or holding a conversation in a crowded and noisy room.

I'm always attracted to moving images. If there's a television screen with a moving image in my field of vision, I can't seem to keep my attention from wandering to it. And it doesn't matter what's playing. It could be the news, sports, cartoons, or a Spanish-language soap opera. If it's a moving image, I'm interested. I recognize that not everybody has this problem. My wife, Laurel, does not have this problem. If we go out for dinner and there's a television in the restaurant, we've learned to position ourselves so that Laurel faces it and I don't. Too often, we've been in the middle of a serious conversation when suddenly I find that I've been watching *Judge Judy* for the past five minutes.

Our capacity to manage our attention allows us to be with others and to give them the precious gift of our exclusive interest for a time. It is a capacity that can be harnessed or habitually neglected. Turning off your cell phone and removing your dark sunglasses for a personal conversation are acts of courtesy and even love. Nothing says "I couldn't care less" more effectively than the frequent sideways-downward glance in the direction of your front pocket to see who just sent you a text message. We have a fair degree of control over the direction of our attention — and it's a good thing that we do. By managing our attention wisely, we can make ourselves lovingly present for the people with whom we interact.

Even the capacity for procrastination has its role to play in healthy human existence. How often are we saved from embarrassment, and fates much worse, by our ability to refrain from acting on impulse in the moment of conviction? I've often had regrets about acting on impulse; I've rarely had regrets about "sleeping on it." Were we incapable of procrastination of this sort, we would be slaves to the strongest feeling of the moment — for good or for ill.

These capacities that make self-deception possible are to be celebrated. They serve us well when they're properly in use. They make possible for us a rich life of sympathy, focus, and reflective decision-making. Without them, our perspective would be confined, our cognitive functioning chaotic, and our decision-making impulsive. The first step in adopting a balanced perspective on self-deception, then, is to see that the capacities that make it possible are not design flaws. We're not flawed for having these capacities. We are creatures to be wondered at for our complexity.

For all we've said, though, these capacities are like nuclear energy, and self-deception like the nuclear bomb. Nuclear energy, in and of itself, may be a wonderful discovery pregnant with unimaginable potential. But there's nothing good about the bomb. It represents the dangerous side of an otherwise wonderful technology.

So far, it looks like self-deception is just a tragic misappropriation of these otherwise fantastic capacities. The capacities may be good, but there's nothing good about putting them to use in the service of self-deception. Perhaps we'd be better off had we never discovered that nuclear energy could be harnessed to create a bomb. Similarly, perhaps we'd be better off had we never learned to put these capacities to use in the service of self-deception.

Could it be, though, that there is a legitimate place for self-deception itself — not just the capacities that make it possible? Could it be that self-deception is not always a departure from the intended exercise of these capacities — that God gave us these capacities in part to make self-deception a possibility for us? The second step in adopting a balanced perspective on self-deception is to see that it is not an evil in and of itself. It sometimes serves legitimate ends. As it turns out, it is not self-deception itself that is to be deplored, but rather its misappropriation.

A Strange Celebration

Adopting a balanced perspective on self-deception requires a sort of strange celebration. We must see that self-deception is not necessarily the capital offense it is made out to be by those who've overestimated the value of authenticity. In fact, it is sometimes something to be celebrated — an unexpected friend in a time of need.

There are two realities that, if I confronted them in their fullness, would almost certainly destroy me. I've mentioned the first already: the unveiled glory of God. In my present condition, I could not bear to see the face of God and live. Fortunately, God has graciously arranged for the possibility of my meeting him without having to face his glory. The other reality that would undo me if squarely confronted is my own sinful condition. Dallas Willard makes this second point nicely:[2]

> Real spiritual need and change . . . is on the inside, in the hidden area of the life that God sees and that we cannot even see in ourselves without his help. Indeed, in the early stages of spiritual development we could not endure seeing our inner life as it really

2. Dallas Willard, *Renovation of the Heart: Putting on the Character of Christ* (Colorado Springs: NavPress, 2002), p. 79.

is. The possibility of denial and self-deception is something God has made accessible to us, in part to protect us until we begin to seek him. Like the face of the mythical Medusa, our true condition away from God would turn us to stone if we ever fully confronted it. It would drive us mad. He has to help us come to terms with it in ways that will not destroy us outright.

Once again, while the truth is often freeing, it is not always so. The truth can be utterly crippling and life-destroying for the person not positioned to receive it. Through discipleship to Jesus, we position ourselves over time to be capable of handling the truth — perhaps in time, even the *whole* truth. If we are disciples of Jesus, then, we position ourselves to be more and more acquainted with the truth — and to experience the truth as freeing. In the meantime, though, God has mercifully designed us with the capacity to avoid and resist truths that we can't handle.

We're really quite used to this idea in our interactions with others. Suppose I learn that your sixteen-year-old son has been smoking pot. I pick up the phone to call you and break the news. I don't want to. But I love you and I love your son. So I'm going to tell you this hard thing, and we're going to walk through it together as best we can. You pick up the phone in tears, hardly able to talk. Before I can even broach the topic of your son, you tell me that your wife has left you for another man. You tell me that you're in utter despair, that you've been drinking, and that you've unlocked the gun cabinet. You just can't think of a single reason to go on living. Clearly this is no time to carry on with my plan to break the news about your son. Someday you'll need to come to grips with the truth about your son. But not today. Not now. I certainly won't bring up the subject of your son. And if you ask questions that might lead us down the path of a conversation about drugs and your son, I'll evade. I'll try to change the subject. I'll do anything to keep *that* subject off the table for now.

There's a time and place for everything, and a fair bit of what makes for a wise counselor is the ability to discern the time and place for truth-telling. Jesus warned of throwing pearls to swine lest they turn on you and tear you to pieces. Often we're so busy blessing our brothers and sisters with our pearls of wisdom that we forget to consider whether they're well positioned to receive them — whether or not a particular person is positioned well to hear a particular truth. The result is often just the one Jesus predicts. We wonder why we're thanked for our truth-telling with vitriol, resentment, and rage. The wise counselor is gracious not only in his tone but also in his timing. Not all truths are for right now.

In his wisdom, God has given me the capacity to be similarly gracious with *myself*. There are truths which I'll have to come to grips with someday but which would completely undo me today. So I deceive myself. I don't approach the subject, and if it's foisted upon me, I evade. I change the subject. I redirect attention. I switch perspectives. I do anything I have to in order to keep *that* subject off the table for now. And it's no small bit of grace on God's part that he's given me the capacity to do so.

Strangely, then, this capacity to evade painful truths — to be self-deceived — is God's gift to us so that we can be as gracious with ourselves as we are — or should be, anyway — with others. It is to be celebrated every bit as much as is the ability of the wise counselor to know when the unveiling of a painful truth will be just too much to bear. It is an unexpected and surprising friend in time of trouble. And in celebrating this friend, we break free of the temptation to think that the ability to deceive oneself is a weakness

— or that it is indicative of some character flaw. Once we see that we were *designed* to have the capacity for self-deception, perhaps there will be less shame in the admission that we *are* in fact self-deceived. And once we're more comfortable with admitting that we are self-deceived, we may be better positioned to recognize those instances in which self-deception has gone astray.

And, to be sure, it does go astray. While we might celebrate the ability of the terminal cancer patient to persist in the unjustified belief that she'll be healed, we do not celebrate the ability to avoid honest reflection on our own mundane shortcomings, the ability to mishandle evidence for our religious commitments, or the ability to be blind to our own materialistic lifestyle. We don't celebrate the ability to evade assistance to the poor through procrastination and attention-management; nor do we celebrate the fact that groupthink often causes us to ignore obvious evidence and mistreat those who disagree with us. Having progressed to the point where we can countenance the possibility that we are self-deceived, then, we must think carefully about how to detect it where and when it occurs and how to take steps away from it when it's not helping us.

CHAPTER 7

How-Not-To, Part 2:
Three Good Ideas

A Word About Freud

W HEN IT COMES TO doing battle with self-deception, one tempting suggestion comes to us from Sigmund Freud's discovery of psychoanalysis around the turn of the twentieth century. Disillusioned with hypnosis as a strategy for healing his neurotic patients, Freud experimented with the "talking cure." By drawing his patients into conversation about their problems and anxieties, he sought to unearth negative emotional energy that the unconscious self had repressed and veiled from the patient's conscious awareness. The goal of psychoanalysis was to draw attention to these repressed thoughts and feelings in order to rid them of their distorting and disorientating power.

A hundred years later, talk of psychotherapy, repression, and unconscious thoughts and desires is familiar to educated and introspective people. We've grown accustomed to the idea that there is, in addition to the self we all know and love, a second center of intention that works behind a curtain of sorts. This second self is alarmingly clever, is perfectly camouflaged, never sleeps, and has virtually unlimited access to the levers that control our conscious experience. A scary creature, really.

By acquainting us with this second self, though, Freud gave us a convenient way of talking about self-deception — as well as a natural suggestion as to how to be rid of it. For the Freudian, self-deception occurs whenever this second self deceives the self we all know and love. It filters perception, blocks things from view, and distorts memory. It does anything it has to do to get the conscious self believing whatever it is that it wants the conscious self to believe. The corresponding suggestion as to how to move past self-deception is to get yourself into psychotherapy. The psychotherapist has unique training that allows her to expose the machinations of this second self. And once it's exposed, we can introduce counter-measures.[1]

Now this isn't the place for a critical discussion of Freud's views. No doubt there is much about me that falls beyond the pale of my possible awareness. But the kinds of self-deceptive strategies I've been discussing — many of them, anyway — are not undertaken unconsciously in Freud's sense. They occur, rather, on the periphery of conscious awareness. We're aware of them, but only just barely. They're like the low constant hum of the air-conditioner in my office. As soon as someone mentions it, I can hear it — and I'm aware that I've been hearing it all along. It moves in and out of the center of my conscious awareness, but I'm never altogether unaware of it — and it's certainly not beyond the pale of my *possible* awareness. I can direct my attention to it at any time. I suspect there is great value for some in psychoanalysis.

---

1. See Daniel Goleman, *Vital Lies, Simple Truths: The Psychology of Self-Deception* (New York: Simon and Schuster, 1985) for the clearest example of a discussion of self-deception in explicitly Freudian terms.

It is not, however, the *primary* cure for the kinds of self-deception we've been discussing.

And wouldn't it be strange if it *were?*

Insofar as it's a vice, self-deception is a very old vice. It's an old vice for people generally. It's an old vice for Christians. People have been aware of it for as long as they've been self-aware. And Christians have been aware of its negative impact on the pursuit of God for as long as there have been Christians.

What a shock it would be, then, if the primary strategy for doing battle with the negative effects of self-deception were altogether unavailable until Freud's discovery of psychoanalysis late in the nineteenth century! To emphasize psychoanalysis as the primary strategy for moving out of self-deception is to imply that the vast majority of people who have ever lived (and the vast majority of people living now, for that matter) are virtually powerless against it. Maybe that's true. I certainly haven't argued that it's not. But it would be surprising if it were. Is it plausible that God would bless us with this capacity for self-deception but leave almost everyone virtually powerless against its vicious misappropriation? In any case, wise people down through the ages who've not been acquainted with psychoanalysis have *not* considered themselves powerless against it. Whatever the value of psychoanalysis, then, we will set it aside for now in order to explore a couple of strategies for moving out of self-deception that are, and always have been, available to just about everybody — even those without access to assistance from a trained psychoanalyst.

I don't know that there's anything like a "cure" for self-deception. If there is, I surely haven't discovered it. What follows, though, are some good ideas about how to make progress on moving out of it.

Good Idea #1: Die

Self-deception is almost never an end in itself. People do not employ self-deceptive strategies simply for the sake of being self-deceived. Self-deception always serves some other purpose — sheer survival, escaping from painful truths, avoiding painful self-knowledge, evading moral conviction. The list could go on and on.

Often, self-deception is an essential ingredient in the recipe for persisting in habitual or secret sin. Most hypocrisy is coupled with self-deception, because we don't like to think of ourselves as duplicitous. Occasionally you come across those who, like Shakespeare's Iago or Dumas's Edmond Dantes, are capable of extended and fully self-conscious deception of others. They can engage in pure deception without any need of thinking that they're doing anything to the contrary. Most of us, though, find it difficult to live with the thought that we are presenting a false self for others. So we employ self-deceptive strategies — and are, as a result, taken in with everyone else by the presentation of this false self.

The way of Jesus is the way of the cross. It is the way of death to self and rebirth to a life caught up in the abundant and joyously unselfish experience of the Trinitarian community of God. You simply can't read Jesus honestly and come away with the idea that he'll take half of you and leave the other half to be governed by whatever it is that presently runs the show. We must decide to die to whatever program we had running before we met him if we're to be his disciples.

In particular, you must decide to die to whatever sin has hold of you. For many, this will mean deciding to die to various addictions — to money, to possessions, to sexual gratification, to attention, to professional success, to habitual anger, to contempt, to arrogance. This is not to say that you have to be dead to these things before you can follow Jesus. It is to say that you must have *decided* to be dead to them. You must be *dying* to them.

This process of dying to self may take a lifetime. But to crucify something is to have put a plan into action that will affect the death of whatever it is that is being crucified. Paul says that he has been crucified with Christ. Paul was not dead to himself. He continued to struggle against his flesh. But he had been crucified. He was in the process of dying to self and living — really living.

If there is anything I've not crucified for the sake of following Jesus, then I'll have just a few relatively unattractive options when it comes to my own self-conception. First, I can simply admit that I've not yet taken up the invitation to be a disciple of Jesus in the sense described in the Gospels. But, one might think, that's tantamount to saying I'm not a Christian! And admitting *that* to myself and others will mean squaring up to some fairly weighty costs both in this life and the next.

Second, I can convince myself that it's possible to be a disciple of Jesus without dying to self. This will require self-deception. I'll need to find my way into a reading of Scripture according to which God is willing to share the throne of my life with my obsession with body image or my addiction to attention and praise. Needless to say, I'll need to manage my attention very carefully as I approach the Scriptures in order to keep that illusion going.

Third, I can convince myself that I really have crucified these addictions when I have not. But this too will require self-deception. If I've not crucified these addictions, that will be a manifest truth over time. Once again, to crucify something is to put a plan into action that will affect its death. In general, it is clear — given enough time — whether or not something is dying. This is true whether the thing in question is a dog, a relationship, or a sinful habit.

Of course, crucifying an addiction will rarely result immediately in the disappearance of the addiction. If I've crucified my addiction to heroin, I've put a plan into action which will affect the death of my addiction. I may still be addicted — I may even have used recently — but a plan is in place to rid me of my addiction over time. If, in five years, I'm still getting the shakes if I go more than a couple of days without a fix, then I did not crucify the addiction. Likely, this will be either because I never really intended to, or because my plan was ineffective. If I discover that my plan has been ineffective and I've really intended to crucify the addiction, I'll revise or replace the plan and start right in again.

Likewise, if I'm as addicted to praise now as I was ten years ago, then it's a fair bet that I did not crucify my addiction to praise ten years ago. Either I never really intended to, or my plan for crucifying that addiction was an ineffective one. But if I'm going to persist in the belief that I really did crucify that addiction ten years ago and that my current plan for carrying out that crucifixion is a good one, I'll need to ignore all of the obvious evidence that I'm as addicted to praise now as I was then.[2]

If I'm going to be a disciple of Jesus, then, I'm going to be dying. I'm going to be crucified for the sake of being caught up in the glorious life for which I was intended. If I'm not dying, that will be clear over time. But if I'm not dying and I'm going to continue to think of myself as a disciple, I'll need to be self-deceived

---

2. For an excellent discussion of the role of intention in the Christian life, see William Law's 1729 classic *A Serious Call to a Devout and Holy Life*. The first two chapters argue that most who fail to make progress toward holiness fail for simple lack of a genuine intention to do so.

either about the call of the disciple to die or about the fact that I'm not dying. Self-deception affords me the opportunity to enjoy the thought of myself as a disciple without all of the painful business of death and dying.

If, on the other hand, we are dying to self, we will find that the need for self-deception dissipates over time. We'll not need to deceive ourselves about the call of the disciple to die to self, since we'll have heeded that call. We'll not need to deceive ourselves about the degree to which we're not yet dead, since we'll also be aware of the degree to which we *have in fact* died.

So let's not merely use the spiritual *language* of the cross and self-mortification. Let's adopt proven and effective plans for putting to death the various addictions that prevent us from moving more fully into the life of Jesus. Let us move out of the darkness and into the light with respect to our sin. The less we have to hide from ourselves and others, the less we'll be moved in the direction of self-deception.

What sort of plan? Try this. Got a secret sin? Confess it. Choose a trusted friend or small group of friends whom you're pretty sure will continue to love you no matter what they learn. Then tell them. Tell them the whole truth as best you can. Don't whitewash it. Don't try to make it better — or worse — than it is. Just give them an accurate picture of the inner state of your self. Declare to them and God your intention to put to death this sin in your members. Then adopt a realistic plan. Seek counsel from others who've found their way out of your particular situation. You're not the first to have the struggles you're having, and you won't be the last. Then take the first steps. When you fail — you will almost certainly fail — confess your failure. Examine your plan to see if it can be refined in such a way as to make failure less likely.

And keep going. If you go for years and years with no noticeable progress, take a good, hard, critical look at your plan, and have the humility to consider revisions. Don't give up. Remember that God loves you as much when you're failing as he will when you're one day perfected. Not an ounce less. And keep going.

Over time, as you die little by little to the sin that has had hold of you for so long, you'll find yourself less and less inclined to adopt self-deceptive strategies to make life livable. It'll be easier to live with the truth that you're addicted to praise and attention when you're also able to see that you're slightly less addicted than you were five years ago. Maybe a trusted friend sharing your journey will say something like this: "I noticed that you passed up on the opportunity to be noticed in conversation just a few minutes back. Five years ago, you would have jumped into that conversation aggressively because of the attention you'd have received. I think you're making real progress!" Not only will it be easier to live with the truth that you're not perfect, it will be easier to live with the fact that there ought to be noticeable progress toward holiness for those following after Jesus. Though you'll be painfully aware that you're not perfect, you won't need to avoid those passages of Scripture suggesting that significant progress is to be expected for followers of Jesus, because you will have noticed progress in your own case.

This first strategy for dealing with self-deception is indirect. We do battle with self-deception, in part, by eliminating those aspects of our lives which require it. Christians with secret or habitual sins they've no intention of giving up will almost certainly have fallen into hypocrisy. And nothing makes it easier to live with one's hypocritical self than a little self-deception. Reduce the need for self-deception, then, by dying.

Good Idea #2: Groups without Groupthink

As we saw in chapter five, our social group can be our accomplice in self-deception. Often communities fall into dysfunctional patterns of groupthink that reinforce individual self-deceptive efforts. So finding your way into a group is no reliable antidote to self-deception. Still, though, finding your way into a particular kind of group can help tremendously.

What kind? Recall Irving Janis's warning signs of groupthink introduced in chapter five. By reflecting on this list with your group, you might find yourself less likely to fall blindly into the phenomenon.

First, groups infected by groupthink tend to exhibit illusions of invulnerability and unanimity. They believe so strongly in the group's inherent morality that they tend to ignore the ethical or moral consequences of their decisions. A healthy group, on the other hand, has a realistic sense of its own limitations and vulnerability. Its existence is not threatened when its members disagree. And, while it may be united by a common cause, its members have a sensible view of the relative worth of that cause as compared with other goods. If, for example, it is a group united for the purpose of advocating to the church board a worship service that places more emphasis on traditional hymns, its members will recognize that this cause does not justify the character assassination of the worship leader.

Second, groups infected by groupthink tend to have negative and stereotyped views of out-groups. They exert subtle pressure on their members to keep dissenting opinions and arguments to themselves — often by vilifying those with divergent views. To express disagreement is to risk being perceived as one of the vilified "others." The result is a kind of self-censorship that preserves the illusion of unanimity and prevents critical and reflective thought.

For most of my life, I've moved primarily in religiously and politically conservative circles — circles in which questions like "Can you be a Christian and a Clinton supporter?" or "Can you be a Christian and a Democrat?" can be seriously entertained. Even those who have enough sense to answer in the affirmative sometimes express bewilderment that those on the other side haven't noticed the obvious incongruity of their views. They use the word "liberal" as though it were slightly off-color. Often they lower their voice when they use it to describe someone, in the kind of hushed tones they might use to say something really scandalous.

I'm embarrassed to say that it wasn't until sometime in my twenties that it really dawned on me that there were devoted Christians in exactly the opposite camp. I remember vividly a conversation with my cousin Brad on a hike in the Sespe Wilderness. We were talking about big topics like theology, apologetics, biblical interpretation, and the relationship between faith and reason. He casually and seemingly without any embarrassment at all referred to himself and others like him as "liberal Christians." It sounded so strange. Didn't he know that "liberal" was synonymous either with "backslidden," "deeply confused" or at least "worldly"?

Turns out, there are lots and lots of Christians for whom the following are live questions: "Can you be a Christian and a supporter of George W. Bush?" or "Can you be a Christian without also being an environmental activist?" Even those with enough sense to answer in the affirmative sometimes wonder how it is that those on the other side can be so blind to the obvious incongruity of their views. For my liberal friends, "conservative" sounds every bit as negative as does "liberal" in the ears of my conservative friends.

To the degree that conservatives group only with other conservatives, it's likely that they'll continue to vilify their liberal brothers and sisters. Of course the same is true in the other direction. Stereotyped views of the "other" will dominate, and self-critical reflection will be stifled by the fear of being assigned the opposing label — "What are you? Some kind of *liberal?!*" On the other hand, when communities are formed under the banner of discipleship to Jesus and sociopolitical and theological differences are preserved (and not set aside, as they too often are in groups that value diversity), there is real hope of meaningful dialogue and progress together toward the truth.

Such communities will be simply impossible, though, if members draw their primary identity from their sociopolitical or theological associations. For such a person, the risk of discovering error is too high. It will be much safer to band together with those who already agree than to risk identity crisis. These communities must be places where the grace, love, and forgiveness of Christ flows so freely between members that finding that you're wrong is a cause for celebration rather than defense. We're all wrong about any number of things, after all — and if you think you're an exception, this book is especially for you! To discover a mistake that can be corrected should be a joyous and sought-after occasion — not an occasion for the stubborn digging in of heels, especially if we really do care about the truth. But it will not be a joyous occasion unless one feels perfectly safe, loved, and accepted quite independently of one's views.

Groups without groupthink, then, are groups that invite, pursue, and celebrate diversity — not because of some vague commitment to political correctness but because of a heartfelt desire to make progress toward the truth. The occasion to have a safe and thoughtful discussion with someone who genuinely loves you and disagrees with you passionately is a rare and precious gift. These occasions are among our most effective resources for unearthing our unquestioned assumptions and seeing a bigger picture. But all too often these resources are squandered because of discomfort with disagreement and the need to have one's existing views vindicated.

For this reason, ecumenical movements are to be applauded — if they are of the sort that nurture communities of unified disagreement. This is true ecumenism. It seeks not to be rid of disagreement, but to be undivided by our disagreements. We should celebrate and support truly ecumenical movements, not because we wish to be rid of disagreement, but because we'll be best positioned to profit from our disagreements if we're unified in loving communities of discipleship to Jesus.

In a sense, radical pluralists make the same mistake as those who isolate themselves according to a strict set of beliefs: they're both running from disagreement. The isolationists avoid disagreement by creating communities defined precisely by their agreement to various points of theological theory and practice; the pluralists avoid disagreement by resisting commitment to any truth that would imply that others are wrong in what they believe. Sufficiently distanced from those who disagree, each side can safely vilify the "other." The pluralists vilify the isolationists, and the isolationists vilify the pluralists.

All of this vilification would come far less easily, however, if the "others" were among those with whom we regularly ate, joked, played, worshiped, suffered, cried, served the poor, raised our children — and, of course, argued about our disagreements. People with whom you're doing these things are not "others" at all. They're family.

Civilized and polite conversation with people who disagree with you, while good, is far too modest a goal. You can be in civilized and polite conversation with people for whom you have little or no respect. You can have nothing but condescension and contempt in your heart for them even as you engage them with a winsome tone in polite conversation. The "other" is still an alien, even if we're treating him kindly. And conversation with an alien is unlikely to help you discover your own blind spots and unquestioned assumptions. You're more likely to dismiss and condescend than to take to heart whatever she has to offer.

Groups likely to be helpful in the fight against self-deception will be diverse. They won't just be *in conversation* with folks who disagree. They'll be *comprised* of people who disagree.

There will be limits, of course. There will be some disagreements that preclude life together as disciples of Jesus. But the sheer number of Protestant denominations in existence — and the routine hostility between them — suggests that we've radically overestimated the number of such disagreements.

The second good idea, then, for warding off self-deception is to form safe, diverse communities of grace united by a common intention to be disciples of Jesus.

Good Idea #3: The Community of the Holy Spirit

But even our best attempts at community are bound to be imperfect at best. I don't know anyone with friends who hasn't been disappointed by friends. We will fail each other. We'll fail to have the courage to challenge each other, or the grace to do so in helpful ways. We'll fail to see sufficiently clearly into one another's sin and dysfunction. We'll fail to have the endurance to stand with each other in times of need. We'll fail to forgive, to love, to extend grace, and to put our brothers and sisters before ourselves. We will fail each other in these and countless other ways.

Finally, then, my deepest source of rescue from my own self-deceptive wiles is to be found in the promise that God's Spirit is with me to strengthen and help me. For anyone who takes up the way of Jesus, there is the promise that the very Spirit of God will be an interactive presence — the person and voice of God with me everywhere and always. Who better to see through my deceptive techniques, to confront me with the hard truths about myself, to see through my defensive strategies? Who better to love me perfectly even when I disagree, dig in my heels, and defend needlessly? A moment's thought makes it more or less obvious that community with God through the indwelling of the Holy Spirit is, by far, the most important thing I've got going for me when it comes to finding my way out of self-deception. I have unfettered access to the one community of persons in existence who knows me better than any other — indeed, better than I know myself.

This amazing truth will be nothing more than an empty platitude, however, if it is not a part of the lived experience of one's actual life. Mere cognitive affirmation of the indwelling presence of the Holy Spirit will not result in joyous and healing relationship with God's Spirit any more than a mere cognitive affirmation of the presence of chocolate cake in the room will result in a joyous experience of the cake. To enjoy fully the benefits of the cake, you've got to *do* something — several things, really. At the very least, you've got to walk over to the cake, take a bite, and attend to your experience as you eat it.

The same is true of relationships generally. As any neglected spouse will tell you, living in the same house with someone who is available to you for relationship is not the same thing as being in relationship. To enjoy the benefits of genuine relationship with someone, you must *do* something — several things, really. You must move toward them and make yourself available to them. You must present yourself — make yourself present. You must take the time to partake of their unique and life-giving presence in your experience. Finally, attending to your experience as you find intimacy together will give you an appreciation of the redeeming effect of the other. When I write letters to my wife, Laurel, they are often filled with reflections on my own experience of her presence with me. I try hard to articulate the respects in which I'm positively affected by her love. I'm convinced that the writing of these notes does as much for me as it does for her. By attending to my experience as her beloved, I find my way more deeply into the life God has for me with her as my partner.

The doctrine of the indwelling of the Holy Spirit is an invitation to relationship with the Spirit of the Master of the universe. It is the truth — at once both unsettling and deeply hopeful — that for disciples of Jesus, God is always in the room. He stands ready to be in relationship with us. We are free to move into greater and greater depths of relationship with him — or not to.

If I am to enjoy fully the benefits of relationship with him, though, I must *do* something — several things, really. I must move toward him and make myself available for interaction and relationship. I must present myself — make myself present — and I must stand ready to partake of the life-giving presence of God's Spirit with me. Finally, I must take the time to attend to my experience as God's beloved. What has it been like to be with God's Spirit in this encounter? What did I experience? What did

I not experience? Was it exhilarating? Disappointing? Strengthening? Boring? What?

Significant relationship — whether it's with a friend, a spouse, or God's Spirit — doesn't happen automatically. It must be pursued, and it must be pursued from both sides. If you're like most, the number-one enemy of relationship — any relationship — is busyness. Often what prevents me from being present with Laurel in the way I'm describing is the simple fact that I'm busy and in a hurry. I'm physically in the house, but I'm racing from task to task — barely aware that she's in the room at all. I experience her most fully when I've explicitly set aside time for the purpose of being with her.

The indwelling of God's Spirit is the truth that God's always in the room. On rare occasions, he may have a reason forcibly to make his presence known — think of Paul on the road to Damascus, for example. But this is not God's way generally. Generally, God will wait patiently until we are ready to move toward him, partake of his life-giving presence, and reflect on our experience as we do.

This is an extremely attractive feature of God's character, when you stop to think of it. How do you react to people who insist on being noticed whether or not others in the room care to notice them? We think of them as obtrusive, obnoxious, and insecure — even if the message they're breaking in with is a good one.

So God is available for those who pursue him in the way that relationships are generally pursued. Wise Christians throughout the ages have recognized the need to schedule time to be with God, even though God is always there. The classical disciplines of silence and solitude are means of securing the space needed to engage meaningfully with God's Spirit. When you care to be with someone, you make space in your calendar, you speak openly, and you listen. Occasionally, you might plan an extended vacation just to be together and enjoy one another's company. Sometimes you simply sit in silence together.

Prayer is my side of the cooperative activity of being together with God. I make space. I tell God what's on my mind and I sit quietly to listen. Sometimes we sit in silence together — neither of us speaking. This all sounds so simple — so trite. But it's far from trite, and if you try it for a reasonable period of time — really try it — you'll find that God is ready to meet with you.

Sometimes the simplest and most obviously sound advice is the least often heeded. It's a little like telling someone who wants to lose a few pounds that they should try eating less and exercising more. It's not that the simple advice has been tried and found wanting so much as that it is rarely tried — at least not tried for a long enough period of time to be realistically effective. It's easy to find people who've altered diet and exercise for a week or a month without noticeable results. But extremely rare is the person who sticks with the program — really sticks to it — for three years to no avail.

The same is true with the simple plan to spend time alone with God's Spirit and away from the distractions of "ordinary" life. With very few exceptions, people who make a plan to be regularly with God find that he is available to be met with. There is no magic formula when it comes to the use of this time. In my experience, quiet reflection on the Psalms or other well-rehearsed passages of Scripture are good places to start. But this is not the place to attempt detailed instruction for times of solitude with God's Spirit. Several authors have done that better than I possibly could here.[3]

3. As a start, let me just recommend two books that have affected my prayer life as much as any others: Richard Foster's *Prayer: Finding the Heart's True Home* (San Francisco: HarperSanFrancisco, 1992), and Dallas Willard's *The Spirit of the Disciplines* (San Francisco: HarperSanFrancisco, 1990).

Let's return to our problem. I want to move out of those self-deceptive strategies which are not in the service of legitimate ends. I want to know the truth and to experience the freedom to see myself and my world for what it is. But I need help. If I'm in the right sort of community, I can look to my brothers and sisters for correction. But they're limited. And, worse, they might be caught up in the same kinds of self-deception that blind me. But neither is true of God's Spirit. I have it available to me to walk into an interactive relationship with a person of unimaginable strength, knowledge, and wisdom. As a part of my ongoing conversation with him, I am invited to make something like the following request: God, if there is something I've been refusing to see, and it wouldn't undo me to see it, would you please reveal it to me? I have made this request on several occasions and have had it answered in the affirmative. On a few occasions, a thought has occurred to me right there on the spot. More often, though, the prayer has been answered in the voice of trusted friends who've found themselves with things they think they should tell me.

I should add that there are also times in my experience when nothing comes of the request — no new thought, no insight from trusted friends . . . nothing. When that happens, I simply press on with whatever course seems best to me at the time, trusting that, were irredeemable disaster imminent, God would step in for my good. It may be that I'm seeing everything just as it is, and no correction is needed. It may be that I'm not ready yet to handle the truth concerning the issue I'm dealing with. Or it may be that God wishes for me to discover the truth in some other way. Whatever the case, I can be sure that he's working things together for my good and that he is guiding me — over time — in the direction of truth and freedom.

Here then, are three good ideas for making progress out of self-deception. First, die. Take concrete steps to put to death those aspects of your character that make self-deception a necessity. Second, find your way into a diverse community of disciples to Jesus. Make sure it's a group that invites disagreement and critical self-reflection. Third, make a plan to pursue relationship with the one who knows you more fully than you know yourself. Set aside regular times to approach the Spirit of God, set your heart out as honestly as possible before him, listen for his voice, and reflect on your experience as you do.

This is not a cure. For one thing, we are not looking to be cured of our capacity for self-deception, since self-deception is sometimes exactly what we need. What we're looking for is a strategy for moving away from the misuse of this capacity, and these are proven strategies for doing so. If we adopt a balanced view of self-deception, take proven steps toward death-to-self and pursue relationship with a diverse community of other disciples and with God's Spirit, we will find our way progressively into the truth, and we will experience the freedom Christ promises. Not immediately. Perhaps not completely. But significantly and noticeably. And noticeable significant progress toward truth and freedom is a source of deep joy and peace for all who find their way into it.

CHAPTER 8

Three Warnings

S ELF-DECEPTION IS A DANGEROUS topic. The more you think about it and learn about it, the more likely you are to notice it. And, typically, noticing it is not the most pleasant of experiences. Thinkers who've emphasized self-deception in their work — Sartre, Nietzsche, Kierkegaard — have not tended to be the cheeriest of writers. In fact, they're often downright depressing.

Why?

Topics of inquiry, many of them anyway, carry inherent risks. People who make a study of the vast reaches of the cosmos run the risk of losing their grip on the significance of the story being played out on this little speck of space-time we call Earth. Those who make a study of the world's many religions sometimes lose any sense of particular allegiance to the tradition from which they embarked — whatever tradition that was. People who study theology run the risk of reducing God to a system. Those who study apologetics have been known to exaggerate the place of the intellect both in typical conversion experiences and in the faithful pursuit of Jesus.

None of these errors is inevitable. To recognize that an inquiry carries with it a particular kind of risk is *not* to have discovered a decisive reason to resist inquiry. Plenty of those who study theology, for example, avoid the reduction of God to a system. Many who study apologetics avoid undue elevation of the intellect *vis-à-vis* the emotions and the many other aspects of the human experience. Still, the risks are there, and it's a good idea to be aware of them.

Our topic is no different. So our inquiry regarding self-deception in Christian culture concludes with three warnings. Below are three mistakes it would be easy to make with an increased awareness of and knowledge about self-deception. Like the other mistakes we've mentioned, they're avoidable. Like most other hazards, though, you're far less likely to find your way into them if you're aware of them as you go.

Warning #1: Beware of Hyper-Authenticity

Hyper-authentic people are those committed to the faithful expression of whatever is in their heart at any given time, no matter the circumstances. Hyper-authenticity is exactly the opposite of hypocrisy and often comes as an overreaction to it. Hyper-authentic people are fed up with faking and with fakers. They do what they feel like doing, and they say what they think. You never have to wonder whether or not the hyper-authentic person is doing something just to please you, satisfy social expectations, make you comfortable, or set people at ease. If you get a compliment from a hyper-authentic person, take heart: it's nothing short of absolutely sincere. But if you've managed to offend him, well . . . you'd better take cover.

Having been exposed to the harmful and sometimes ridiculous effects of self-deception, it's easy to lapse into a commitment to hyper-authenticity. "Enough of self-deception and pretense," you might say. "I will be absolutely true to myself and to others. I will be for myself and for others exactly who I am. It may be painful sometimes. It may be painful for me, and it may be painful for those around me. But it will be true. No façade. No make-believe."

Big mistake.

Sometimes Laurel and I have fun assigning people nicknames. We generally keep them to ourselves, and they're usually not very creative — names like "Loud Guy" or "Cell Phone Girl" are characteristic. When we have a night out, we often go to dinner at a bistro near home, with a big outdoor patio on a promenade — perfect for people-watching and name-calling.

There our favorite waiter is the one we like to call "Gesticulating Waiter." We call him that because he so perfectly exaggerates all of the body movements associated with being a waiter. In any other setting, his behavior would be utterly obnoxious and annoying. But as a waiter, he's perfect. It's tempting to make unnecessary requests of Gesticulating Waiter — more water, another lemon, an extra plate — just to watch him work.

In his discussion of "bad faith," or the failure to be authentic, Sartre describes Gesticulating Waiter perfectly:

> Let us consider this waiter in the café. His movement is quick and forward, a little too precise, a little too rapid. He comes toward the patrons with a step a little too quick. He bends forward a little too eagerly; his voice, his eyes express an interest a little too solicitous for the order of the customer. Finally there he returns, trying to imitate in his walk the inflexible stiffness of some kind of automaton while carrying his tray with the recklessness of a tight-rope-walker by putting it in a perpetually unstable, perpetu-

ally broken equilibrium which he perpetually re-establishes by a light movement of the arm and hand.

Sartre goes on to explain that all of this seems to us like a game — a performance of sorts. It is not authentic. It is not who he is. It's a role he's put on. "But what is he playing?" Sartre asks. "We need not watch long before we can explain it: he is playing at *being* a waiter in a café . . . the waiter in the café plays with his condition in order to *realize* it."[1]

But here is the paradox: he's playing at being a waiter, but he *is* a waiter, so how is this inauthentic? It's inauthentic precisely because *being* a waiter is something he must *put on*. It is not an expression of his real being. It is artificial, unnatural, and foreign to him. Yet his trade requires that he realize this archetype. Interestingly, the longer he plays at being a waiter, the less unnatural and foreign to him it becomes.

The hyper-authentic person makes a terrible waiter. She refuses to play at *being* a waiter. She simply allows whatever is going on inside to manifest itself to her customers as she discharges her obligation to take orders and deliver food. If she's depressed, she slumps. If she's obsessing about a recent fight with her boyfriend, her patrons know all about it. If she's feeling giddy and chatty, you can't get rid of her. If she's in a quiet mood, she's nowhere to be found. She simply is who she is. No pretense. No deceit. No façade. No tip.

Jesus was down on hypocrisy — he didn't seem to have much room for it at all. As followers of Jesus, we're called to live lives of

---

1. Jean-Paul Sartre, *Being and Nothingness: An Essay on Phenomenological Ontology* (New York: Routledge, 2003), pp. 101-2.

authenticity and candor. At the same time, though, we're called to a lifestyle of imitation. We are imitators of Jesus.

Think about imitation.

When I imitate something or someone, I adopt patterns of being that are external to me, foreign, and unnatural. The presumption of the New Testament is that I do not presently have the character of Christ. Instead, I am twisted and broken. My present opportunity is to play at having the heart of Christ — to imitate him — in an attempt to cooperate with the Holy Spirit as Christ is *realized* in me. With the help of God's Spirit, I put off the old self, that which is authentically me at present, and put on the new self, that which is authentically Christ. Over time, that which was at first artificial, foreign, and unnatural takes root, and I am transformed. I begin by blessing those who curse me, even though everything in me is pushing a curse through my lips. I'm playing. I'm imitating the one for whom the blessing comes naturally. Over time, with the help of the Holy Spirit, that which was once forced and unnatural becomes the reflex response. I begin by deciding to give when my heart is selfish. I'm playing. I'm imitating the one for whom generosity is instinctive. Over time, with the help of the Holy Spirit, that which was once opposed to my nature becomes natural for me — as it was and is for Jesus. We *play* at being Christ's followers in order to *become* his followers.

But this whole process of transformation through imitation is unavailable to the hyper-authentic. They will bless only when they feel a genuine desire for the well-being of the other. They will give only when they *feel* generous. Hyper-authenticity rules out the possibility of imitating anyone other than yourself — and so it rules out the possibility of cooperating with the Holy Spirit in your own spiritual re-formation by imitating the Master.

When I was in college, I picked up the guitar. I played for years without formal instruction before I finally decided to get some lessons. By that time I had settled into some pretty bad habits. At my first lesson, my teacher positioned my thumb differently on the back of the neck of the guitar. Suddenly, I was completely incapable of playing even the simple things I had played before. I felt awkward and unnatural. But the teacher assured me that if I stuck with it, I'd get used to it and, in time, this new position would free me to reach chords I could never have reached using my old method.

Insofar as I am not yet perfectly like Christ, the imitation of Christ will, at times, feel false, unnatural, and insincere. But if we trust the Master, we'll obey even when obedience isn't what comes naturally — even when obedience runs contrary to what we're feeling at the moment. This isn't hypocrisy; we don't act contrary to our impulses in an attempt to fake anybody out. We act contrary to our impulses because we wish to be re-trained. We wish to be something other than what we are today. We wish to be putting off the old self and putting on the new.

Imitation, then, can be perfectly authentic. It can be the out-working of an authentic intention to take on the heart and character of Christ. But imitation precludes hyper-authenticity. So if you want to be a student of Jesus, beware of hyper-authenticity.

Warning #2: Beware of Undue Suspicion of Self-Deception in Others

"What did you think of the sermon?"
    "I thought it was just great!"

"Yeah, me too. I wish so-and-so had been there. It was exactly what she needs to hear."

I can't tell you how many post-sermon conversations — either with others or with myself — have gone that way in my experience. Somehow, it's so much easier to think of all the *other* people who should have been there to hear the convicting word than it is to receive the convicting word for myself.

It's the same with self-deception. A little knowledge about self-deceptive strategies is all it takes to start noticing it in everyone — everyone *else*, that is. The point of this book is not *primarily* to help you locate, assess, and deal with the self-deception of *others* in your context. The point of this book is to help you locate, assess, and deal with *your own* self-deceptive strategies. So beware of the temptation to think primarily of the others in your experience that should be more aware than they are of their self-deceptive tendencies.

There are two problems with fixating on the self-deceptive strategies of others. The first is that it is a quick recipe for cynicism and, ironically, for deceiving yourself. Nothing is easier than to diagnose disagreement and tension with another person or group in terms of *their* self-deception. What else could possibly explain their seeming inability to see what seems to you so obviously true? Thinking this way will lead quickly to a habitual cynicism about others — especially others with whom you disagree. This cynicism will, in turn, rob you of the joy of community with those who are, in many ways, best suited to help you grow.

Moreover, the thought that the other person is self-deceived can, itself, become a primary strategy for deceiving yourself. If I think you are self-deceived, then I have every reason to disregard or discount your perspective. There's no reason for me to take you seriously, since your take on things is a consequence of your own self-deception.

The thought that you are self-deceived, then, can be an effective aid in attention management. I manage my attention away from you — the one who disagrees — by thinking that you're self-deceived. And in so doing, I safeguard my own cherished perspective from a serious consideration of your critique.

The second problem with fixating on the self-deceptive strategies of others is that I am rarely well-positioned to *do* anything about the self-deception of others — even if I'm right that they're self-deceived. The self-deceiver is deceiving herself for a reason. She's avoiding *something*. And the suggestion that she's self-deceived, if heeded, will of course make her self-deception all that much more difficult. Until she's ready to deal with whatever it is she's avoiding, then, the suggestion that she's self-deceived is likely to be shrugged off. And if she *is* ready to deal with it, then she's probably already moving out of the self-deception — without my help. In either case, the suggestion that someone else is self-deceived is not likely to be very helpful.

There are exceptions, of course. Part of the call of this book is for the formation of safe communities where the reality of self-deception can be openly addressed. In such a community, there is implicit or even explicit permission to point out instances of self-deception in others. In this context of mutual invitation, the suggestion that I'm self-deceived is far less likely to be shrugged off. But typically one will have this kind of safe transparency with a very limited number of people. Beyond the safety of this community of grace, the suggestion that someone else is self-deceived — even if correct — is probably pearls to swine.

Warning #3: Beware of Undue Self-Doubt

There are two errors to be avoided when it comes to self-trust. The first is a kind of unquestioning faith in one's own perspective as an infallible guide to matters of significance. A person who takes this approach acts with unhesitating certainty. He feels no need to get a second opinion and quickly dismisses divergent views as irrelevant. If he's a Christian, perhaps he thinks of himself as needing only to consult Jesus. He resonates strongly with the image of Lucy and Aslan standing alone at the bridge ready to confront all opposing forces in *Prince Caspian*. It's just him and Jesus. The thought that he might be hearing from Jesus only what he wants to hear is not so much as a blip on his radar.

Careful attention to the phenomena discussed in this book will not likely promote this kind of error.

On the other end of the spectrum, though, is the error of undue self-doubt. To fall into this error is to be paralyzed by the thought that you might be self-deceived as you contemplate significant issues. The person undone by self-doubt will rarely have a settled opinion about anything if there's a chance of self-deception. Such people will be incapable of acting on the basis of their own convictions without checking, double-checking, and triple-checking with others.

"But what would you do if you were me, Daddy?" Of late, that is the question my six-year-old son, Silas, asks of me more than any other. He might be trying to choose a flavor of ice cream, which game to play next, or what to say in response to a question. He's a very thoughtful little boy, and he doesn't like making mistakes. He comes by it honestly. Of our two errors, I more frequently fall into this second one. I like the thought of double-checking and triple-checking my work, my opinions, and my decisions with others I respect before I move forward. Sometimes, though, Silas finds himself virtually incapable of moving forward without a concrete answer to his question. If I don't tell him what I'd do in his shoes, he freezes.

It's a good thing to seek a wider perspective from others we respect — and most of all from the Holy Spirit. Sometimes, though, we must simply act on the basis of whatever limited knowledge we possess. To be incapable of doing so is to have fallen into the error of undue self-doubt.

Often I tell Silas what I would do in his shoes, and it's always a tremendously comforting experience for him. He then confidently moves forward in the knowledge that he's on a wise course. Just as often, though, I choose *not* to answer his question. Even if there is an option I know I would take, even if there is an option I think best for him, I let him live through the uncertainty of acting without knowing what Daddy would do. How else will he ever learn to make decisions and live with consequences? In fact, I've found that if I give him a concrete answer too often, he grows more and more dependent and less and less capable of striking out in his own thinking. What I want for Silas is that he grow increasingly capable of wise action without my immediate intervention — that his character mature to the point where wisdom would be its natural course.

When I was a young man, God made it very clear to me in several different ways (among others, a trip to the hospital and reconstructive surgery) that I should not continue my pursuit of a career in law and should instead study philosophy for a season. It was, in some respects, a scary and difficult shift. But there was great comfort in the knowledge that I was acting in obedience to the One who could ultimately care for all of my needs.

Since then, I've often sought the same kind of clear guidance when I've had big decisions to make. On occasion, I've received concrete guidance — though never with the degree of clarity with which came the instruction to pursue philosophy. When I have received guidance, it has come in a variety of ways: a passage of Scripture comes alive in a new way, a friend offers a word, a new thought occurs in prayer.

Just as often, though, my Heavenly Father refuses to tell me what he'd do in my shoes. I've come to interpret his silence in these instances as an invitation to grow up. These are opportunities to grow past my self-doubt, to step out into whatever course seems best to me after a responsible inquiry, and to stand with whatever consequences may come. I would never knowingly let Silas make a mistake that would destroy him. I confidently expect the same of my Heavenly Father. He may let me make mistakes. But the great promise of Romans 8 is that he'll not let me do anything that can't be brought around for good.

So we have something of a tightrope to walk. The possibility of self-deception is real, and its consequences are often undesirable. So we should do what we can to broaden our perspective. We must refuse to squander the resources of God's diverse body by adopting a just-me-and-Jesus approach to thinking and decision-making. But we must also live with the fact that self-deception will not always be avoidable. We may find ourselves without the resources for double-checking and triple-checking our convictions, and even God may be silent. Often, in such a case, we must carry on in the world as best we can for the sake of God's kingdom, trusting that he's grand enough to bring beauty from the ashes of our often ill-informed action.

Let us then move forward as best we can with an increased awareness of the patterns of self-deception in our midst. Let us focus most squarely on the manifestations of self-deception in our own experience, lest we become cynical of others. But may we do so without implicitly committing ourselves to hyper-authenticity, which rules out the imitation of Christ, and without undue self-doubt, which robs us of the joy that comes when we act in the world in the authority of Christ for the sake of his kingdom.

Index